The Pig That Wants to Be Eaten

The Pig That Wants to Be Eaten

And ninety-nine other thought experiments

Julian Baggini

Granta Books
London

Granta Publications, 2/3 Hanover Yard, Noel Road, London N1 8BE

First published in Great Britain by Granta Books 2005

A CIP catalogue record for this book is available from the British Library.

7 9 10 8 6

ISBN 1 86207 748 7

Typeset by M Rules

Printed and bound in Great Britain by William Clowes Ltd, Beccles, Suffolk

Contents

Preface

Imagination without reason is mere fancy, but reason without imagination is sterile. That is partly why scientists and philosophers alike have always used imaginary scenarios to help sharpen their ideas and push them to their limits. The purpose of such 'thought experiments' is to strip away the things that complicate matters in real life in order to focus clearly on the essence of a problem.

So, for example, a real-life ethical dilemma will always be complicated by contingent, context-specific factors. Take the general issue of whether eating meat is morally wrong. If you consider whether it is wrong to eat the meat you have an opportunity to consume, multiple factors come into play. Some animals will have been factory farmed, some humanely reared, some caught wild. Some animals will have been raised on land that was once rainforest, others will have freely grazed on open pastures. Some meat will be organic, some will be genetically modified, some will have been shipped from the other side of the world. Deciding the ethical rights and wrongs requires untangling all these multiple factors, and weighing up the different considerations accordingly.

Thought experiments can help because, like scientific experiments, they aim to isolate the key variables, the specific factors under examination, to see what difference they, and they alone, make to our understanding of the world. So if we want to consider the ethics of eating animals we can imagine situations in which the particular issue of concern is the only one to differ between two scenarios. If we're worried about how we treat farm animals, let us imagine what difference good treatment, and good treatment alone, makes. If our intentions are under scrutiny, we can ask what difference does it make if the chicken in your kiev died in an accident whereas mine had its neck wrung intentionally, but before that they had lived identical lives. We can simply stipulate that all other things are equal, so the only question we need to settle is the core moral one.

Thought experiments do not just have the advantage of being tidier than real life. They can actually help us think about things that we could, or would, not test in real life. Sometimes they require us to imagine what is impractical or even impossible, either for us right now or for all people at all times. Although what these experiments ask us to consider can seem outlandish, the purpose is the same as for any thought experiment: to keep our focus on one core concept or problem. If an impossible scenario helps us to do that, then its impossibility need not concern us. The experiment is merely a tool to aid our thinking, it does not pretend to describe actual life.

The 100 scenarios in this book are inspired mostly, but not always, by the arguments of philosophers. Sometimes they take assumptions we rarely question and turn them upside down. Sometimes they suggest ways of resolving what seem to be intractable problems. And sometimes they make us see problems which don't seem like problems at all until you follow through their implications.

This is neither a reference book nor a collection of answers to old puzzles; it is rather a provocation, a stimulus to further thought. In the comments that follow the scenarios, I may suggest a way out of the difficulty or I may be playing devil's advocate: it is for you to decide which.

Similarly, the cross-referencing is intended to be suggestive, not scientific. Sometimes the connections between the scenarios will be obvious. On other occasions the link is itself a means of making you look at the problem in a new light.

Many lines of thought can be started from this book. But none ends in it.

Acknowledgements

Thought experiment number 101: a writer accepts the freely given support, help and advice of others and fails to thank them in the acknowledgements of his book. Is he simply careless and forgetful, or morally culpable?

I am sure I am one or the other. But I won't neglect everyone. Editors, for whom their job title implies a verb and not just a noun, make crucial contributions to how books turn out. George Miller is one such editor, and his input, from conception to completion, has been indispensable. I have also been helped by a number of wonderful people at Granta: Sajidah Ahmad, Louise Campbell, Francis Hollingdale, Gail Lynch, Angela Rose, Will Salmon, Bella Shand, Colette Vella and Sarah Wasley. And Lizzy Kremer continues to guide and support both robustly and shrewdly.

To avoid mentioning some and neglecting others, I'd like to issue blanket thanks to everyone who may have answered a query or provided a source during the writing of this book. To say there are too many to mention would be a lie. There are simply too many for someone not careful enough to keep a record to remember.

Finally, I'd like to thank Jeremy Stangroom, officially because his intelligence, insight and challenging conversation have been an inspiration for several years, but really because he thinks acknowledgements and dedications are more often than not self-aggrandising and ingratiating, so this will really annoy him.

A note on sources

Where there are one or more identifiable sources for an experiment, I have included details of them at the end of the scenario. It should be noted, however, that although my versions are sometimes very similar to those in the source material, on other occasions they are very different. Readers should therefore assume that these sources provide no more than the inspiration for the scenarios in this book.

Where no source is given, it is usually because the thought experiment is inspired by a wider debate in which no one or two sources can be singled out. It should not be taken necessarily to indicate originality on my part.

Some of these scenarios may have sources of which I am unaware and have therefore not credited. I would be happy to rectify any such omissions in any future editions.

1. The evil demon

Is anything so self-evident that it cannot be doubted? Is it not possible that our lives are no more than dreams, or that the world is just a figment of our imaginations? Outlandish though these notions are, the mere fact that they are conceivable shows that the reality of the physical world can be doubted.

There are other ideas, however, which seem to be so clear and self-evident that they must be true. For instance, whether you are awake or asleep, two plus two makes four. A triangle must have three sides whether the world, real or imaginary, contains triangles or not.

But what if God, or some powerful, malicious demon, is tricking you? Couldn't such an evil spirit fool you into believing that the false is obviously true? Haven't we seen hypnotists make people count to ten, unaware that they have missed out the number seven? And what of a man who, in a dream, hears four strikes of the clock tower bell and finds himself thinking, 'How odd. The clock has struck one four times!'

If the evil demon is a possibility, is there anything which is beyond doubt?

Source: The first meditation from *Meditations* by René Descartes (1641)

Philosophers have a habit of finding something we think we all know and then providing reasons for making us doubt we know it after all. Laws of nature, the physical world, God, goodness, other minds, justice, time – philosophers have found reasons to doubt them all.

In order to advance such profoundly sceptical arguments, the philosopher needs to use the one thing he cannot afford to doubt: his own capacity to think rationally. So, for example, the reality of time can be doubted because the traditional concept of time contains contradictions. These contradictions involve a violation of basic logical principles, such as the impossibility of both being and not being at the same time. It is the ability to recognise that these are logical contradictions that allows the philosopher to reason and justify his doubt.

But if we were under the influence of a powerful deceiving demon, a possibility first proposed by the seventeenth-century French philosopher René Descartes, then we might be wrong to take these basic logical principles to be true. It may seem to us that they are obvious and self-evident, but to the person under hypnosis it may seem obvious and self-evident that eight follows six. To the deluded dreamer it may seem obvious and self-evident that the clock has struck one o'clock four times, when we all 'know' it has actually struck four o'clock once.

The idea of a deceiving demon may seem a little extravagant, but the same doubt can be introduced by other means. We could just be mad, and our insanity may blind us to the fact that others do not view the world the way we do. Or perhaps evolution has endowed all of our minds with a fundamentally flawed set of logical principles. Maybe we are better adapted to survival if we take certain falsehoods to be 'obviously true'. The demon may be encoded in our DNA.

The genius of this thought experiment is that, in order to judge its plausibility, we have to rely on the one thing the test is supposed to call into doubt: our capacity to reason well. We have to judge whether we are able to think well by thinking as well as we can. So we cannot set ourselves apart from the faculty of thought we are supposed to be assessing to judge it from a neutral perspective. It is like trying to use a suspect set of scales to weigh itself, in order to test its accuracy.

Perhaps this is the thought experiment's pay-off: our capacity to reason has to be taken as basic for any serious thought to be undertaken at all. We can doubt whether any particular piece of reasoning is sound by thinking hard about it. But we cannot doubt whether our general capacity for reason is flawed or not. At best we can say it seems to serve us well enough. Is that enough to vindicate rationality, or does it leave it weakened?

See also

19. Bursting the soap bubble
28. Nightmare scenario
51. Living in a vat
98. The experience machine

2. Beam me up . . .

For Stelios, the teletransporter is the only way to travel. Previously it took months to get from the Earth to Mars, confined to a cramped spacecraft with a far from perfect safety record. Stelios's TeletransportExpress changed all that. Now the trip takes just minutes, and so far it has been 100 per cent safe.

However, now he is facing a lawsuit from a disgruntled customer who is claiming the company actually killed him. His argument is simple: the teletransporter works by scanning your brain and body cell by cell, destroying them, beaming the information to Mars and reconstructing you there. Although the person on Mars looks, feels and thinks just like a person who has been sent to sleep and zapped across space, the claimant argues that what actually happens is that you are murdered and replaced by a clone.

To Stelios, this sounds absurd. After all, he has taken the teletransporter trip dozens of times, and he doesn't feel dead. Indeed, how can the claimant seriously believe that he has been killed by the process when he is clearly able to take the case to court?

Still, as Stelios entered the teletransporter booth once again and prepared to press the button that would begin to dismantle him, he did, for a second, wonder whether he was about to commit suicide . . .

Source: Chapter 10 of *Reasons and Persons* by Derek Parfit (Oxford University Press, 1984)

On what does our continued survival depend? In normal circumstances, we would say the continued functioning of our body. But since there is no part of the body that couldn't conceivably be replaced by a synthetic substitute, perhaps this is not necessarily true. Isn't it rather that we continue to exist just as long as our consciousness continues? The day no one wakes up thinking he is me, with my memories, plans and personalities, is the day I have died.

The 'psychological continuity' theory of personal identity has an intuitive appeal. It is only because it seems to reflect our fundamental intuitions that we can make sense of stories such as Kafka's *Metamorphosis*, in which a man wakes up in the body of a beetle. We instantly recognise that the man *is* the beetle because his mind inhabits it. Mental, not physical continuity, marks him out as the same person.

But in the case of teletransportation, although we do have psychological continuity as complete as it is in ordinary life, it also seems beyond doubt that what has been created is a copy, a clone. A clone, however, is not the same individual as the person cloned. It is the same only in the sense that two statues cast from the same mould are the same: they are identical in every detail but they are distinct entities nonetheless. If you chip one, the other remains undamaged.

It is not as though Stelios doesn't know how his teletransporter works. He just doesn't see why the fact that, strictly speaking, the machine 'clones' him every time should matter. What matters to him is that, as far as he is concerned, he walks into the booth and wakes up on another planet. The physical mechanism is irrelevant.

If that sounds glib, consider for a moment the possibility that one night, a few years ago, you were kidnapped in your sleep, processed by the teletransporter, and the resulting person returned, unknowing, to your bed. Had this happened, you would have no way of telling, because your conscious experience of your ongoing life as a continuing being would be exactly the same if it had not happened. The fact of teletransportation, in some sense, leaves your life and world exactly as it was.

Perhaps then to ask whether Stelios is a clone or 'the same' person is the wrong question. Perhaps we should instead ask what matters about our past and future existence. And maybe the answer to that is psychological continuity, by whatever means necessary.

See also

38. I am a brain
46. Amoebaesque
65. Soul power
88. Total lack of recall

3. The Indian and the ice

Dhara Gupta lived all her life in a village near Jaisalmer in the Rajastan desert. One day, in 1822, as she was cooking dinner, she became aware of a commotion. She looked up to discover that her cousin, Mahavir, had returned from a trip he had begun two years before. He looked in good health, and over dinner he told them of his adventures.

There were tales of robbers, wild animals, great mountains and other incredible sights and adventures. But what really stunned Dhara was his claim to have seen something called 'ice'.

'I went to regions where it was so cold, the water stopped flowing and formed a solid, translucent block,' said Mahavir. 'What is more amazing is that there is no state in between where the liquid thickens. The water that flows freely is only slightly warmer than that which has solidified.'

Dhara did not want to challenge her cousin in public, but she did not believe him. What he said contradicted all her experience. She did not believe it when travellers told her of fire-breathing dragons. Nor would she believe this nonsense about ice. She rightly thought she was too intelligent for that.

Source: Chapter X 'On Miracles' from *An Essay Concerning Human Understanding* by David Hume (1748)

How could Dhara be right when in one sense she was so obviously wrong? We know that Mahavir's account of ice was not a fantasy on a par with tales of dragons, but an accurate description of what happens to water at freezing point.

Dhara was right in the sense that sometimes we are wrong for the right reasons. Take, for example, get-rich-quick schemes. Most people who use email will receive messages virtually every day promising huge riches for a 'small' capital outlay. Because these are almost without exception frauds and it would take too much time to investigate their credentials one by one, the only rational course of action is to ignore them all. However, that means it is possible that one day you will ignore a genuine opportunity and forgo great wealth. That particular email would not be a fraud, yet in an important sense you would still have reasoned correctly when you concluded it probably was.

The same general point applies to Dhara. We should not believe everything we are told about how the natural world works. When people tell us that they can levitate, stop watches with their minds or cure diseases with crystals we should rightly be sceptical. Our past experience tells us that such events do not happen, and all previous claims that they have occurred have either lacked evidence to back them up or been shown to be fraudulent. We do not need to think that those making the claims are themselves con artists: they may simply be mistaken or basing their claims on bad reasoning.

The problem is, however, that sometimes something genuinely does come along that forces us to reconsider what we thought we knew. We cannot dismiss an idea simply because it doesn't fit with our present beliefs. Rather, we need very good reasons to do so, because what is firm and established has to carry more weight than what is being claimed by an individual or small group which goes against it.

This is where Dhara has a problem. The testimony of one person, even if it is her cousin, is not strong enough to contradict what she knows about the natural world, where liquids do not change to solids at a seemingly magical temperature. Yet she must also accept that she has not been to these colder climes, whereas her cousin has. Her own experience is therefore limited, but she has only her cousin's word about what lies beyond it. By refusing to believe him, did she make the limits of her knowledge too narrow, or was being wrong on this occasion the price she paid for not being gullible and mistaken in many more situations?

See also

40. The rocking-horse winner
63. No know
76. Net head
97. Moral luck

4. A byte on the side

Like many people who had been married for several years, Dick was bored with his relationship. There was no passion these days. In fact, Dick and his wife hardly slept together at all. However, Dick had no intention whatsoever of leaving his wife. He loved her and she was an excellent mother to their children.

He knew full well what the usual solution to this problem was: have an affair. You simply accept that your wife satisfies some of your needs and your mistress others. But Dick really didn't want to go behind his wife's back, and he also knew that she could not deal with an open relationship, even if he could.

So when Dick heard about Byte on the Side Inc. ('Even better than the real thing!'), he had to take it seriously. What the company offered was the opportunity to conduct a virtual affair. Not one-handed cyber sex with a real person at the other end of the computer connection, but a virtual reality environment in which you 'slept with' a completely simulated person. It would feel just like real sex, but, in fact, all your experiences would be caused by computers stimulating your brain to make it seem to you as though you were having sex. All the thrills of an affair, but with no third person, and hence no real infidelity. Why should he say no?

Why does infidelity bother us? Some people say it shouldn't and that it is only because we are culturally conditioned with unrealistic expectations of monogamy that it does. Sex and love are quite different, and we are fools if we allow a bond of affection to be broken by the biologically driven act of copulation.

If the desire for monogamy is an artefact of culture, it is nonetheless very deeply rooted. It is the experience of many who enter free-love communes or try 'swinging' that they just can't help being jealous when others sleep with the one they love. The 'hang ups' we are blithely told to throw away seem to be more than just psychological aberrations to be overcome.

So if infidelity is likely to remain a problem for the majority, what is it about it that bothers us? Imagining how we'd feel about the prospect of our partner using Byte on the Side's services might help us to answer this question. If we would have no objection to the cyber sex, that would suggest that the crucial factor is the involvement of another person. Our most intimate relationship must be one-to-one and exclusive. Traditional monogamy is what we want to see maintained.

But if we would object to the virtual affair, that would seem to indicate that it is not the role of the third party which is crucial after all. What causes the hurt is not the turning *to* someone else, but the turning *away* from the relationship. On this view, when Dick turns on a computer to turn him on, he is signalling that he has stopped seeing his wife as the person with whom he wishes to express his sexuality.

An affair is usually a symptom of a relationship's existing problems, not the first cause of them. This fits this diagnosis of the source of the unease with Dick's virtual lover. For it is of course true, even before he has logged on to his stimulating simulation for the first time, that he has already stopped seeing his wife sexually in the way he once did. And so the virtual affair is not a means of dealing with the core problem, but of avoiding it.

In the real world, the reasons why infidelity bothers us are complex, and the person who objects to a virtual byte on the side may object even more strongly to a flesh and blood affair. What the case of Dick enables us to do is to focus our attention on just one aspect of unfaithfulness: the extent to which it is a turning away from our most valued relationship.

See also

27. Duties done
44. Till death us do part
91. No one gets hurt
96. Family first

5. The pig that wants to be eaten

After forty years of vegetarianism, Max Berger was about to sit down to a feast of pork sausages, crispy bacon and pan-fried chicken breast. Max had always missed the taste of meat, but his principles were stronger than his culinary cravings. But now he was able to eat meat with a clear conscience.

The sausages and bacon had come from a pig called Priscilla he had met the week before. The pig had been genetically engineered to be able to speak and, more importantly, to want to be eaten. Ending up on a human's table was Priscilla's lifetime ambition and she woke up on the day of her slaughter with a keen sense of anticipation. She had told all this to Max just before rushing off to the comfortable and humane slaughterhouse. Having heard her story, Max thought it would be disrespectful *not* to eat her.

The chicken had come from a genetically modified bird which had been 'decerebrated'. In other words, it lived the life of a vegetable, with no awareness of self, environment, pain or pleasure. Killing it was therefore no more barbarous than uprooting a carrot.

Yet as the plate was placed before him, Max felt a twinge of nausea. Was this just a reflex reaction, caused by a lifetime of vegetarianism? Or was it the physical sign of a justifiable psychic distress? Collecting himself, he picked up his knife and fork . . .

Source: *The Restaurant at the End of the Universe* by Douglas Adams (Pan Books, 1980)

Concern for animal welfare is not confined to the small percentage of the population which is vegetarian. This should not be surprising since, if mere killing were the issue, then vegetarians would not swat flies or exterminate rats, which many, though by no means all, are happy to do.

There are two main reasons for maintaining that the rearing and killing of certain animals is wrong. First, there is the issue of the conditions animals are kept in. Here the problem is the alleged misery of an animal while it is alive, rather than the fact of its death. Second is the act of killing itself, which brings to an end the life of a creature which would otherwise have a decent future.

The first issue can be dealt with simply by making sure the animal is kept in good conditions. Many people who are concerned for animal welfare will nonetheless eat meats such as free-range poultry and lamb, which cannot be intensively reared.

However, this still leaves the second rationale for vegetarianism: objection to the act of killing. But what if we could create animals that had no interest in their own survival, simply because they had as little awareness as a carrot? How could it be wrong to deprive them of an existence they never knew they had? Or what if the animal actually wanted to be eaten, such as the bovine imagined by Douglas Adams in *The Restaurant at the End of the Universe*?

The protagonist of that novel, Arthur Dent, recoiled in horror at the suggestion, describing it as 'the most revolting thing I've ever heard'. Many would share his revulsion. But as Zaphod Beeblebrox objected to Dent, surely it's 'better than eating an animal that doesn't want to be eaten'? Dent's response seems to be no more than a version of the 'yuck factor' – the kind of instinctive recoil that people feel when confronted by something that doesn't seem natural, even if there are no moral problems with it. Organ transplants and blood transfusions seemed freakish when first conceived, but as we got used to both, the idea that they are morally wrong has died out, apart from among a few religious sects.

People may talk about the dignity of the animals or of a respect for the natural order, but can we seriously suggest that the dignity of the chicken species is undermined by the creation of a decerebrated version? Isn't Priscilla's death entirely dignified? And aren't even organic arable farmers, who have selected and bred varieties to grow on a mass scale, tampering with the natural order anyway? In short, is there any good reason why the vegetarian of today should not share a table with Max just as soon as his menu becomes a reality?

See also

26. Pain's remains
57. Eating Tiddles
72. Free Percy
91. No one gets hurt

6. Wheel of fortune

Marge was no mathematician, but she knew she had just discovered a foolproof system to get rich playing roulette.

She had been observing the spin of the wheel at the casino for several days. During this time she had noticed that it was surprisingly normal for there to be a sequence of spins when the ball fell into only black or only red slots. But five in a row of the same colour was very unusual and six in a row happened only a couple of times a day.

This was going to be her system. The chances of the ball falling into a slot of the same colour six times in a row were tiny. So, she would watch, and once it fell into, say, red, five times in a row, she would bet that the next one would be black. She was bound to win more often than she lost because six in a row was so rare. She was so confident that she had already started to think about how she would spend the money.

Marge's mistake is a warning against the limits of thought experiments. If her system seems foolproof, it is because she has already tested it out, and it works every time. In her head, that is. If the gambler can be so easily led astray by imagining what would happen in hypothetical situations, so can a philosopher.

Her mistake, however, is one of reasoning, and is not caused by any failure of the real world to match the one of intellect. The mistake she makes is to confuse the probability of the ball falling into the same-colour slot six times in a row with the probability of it falling into the same-colour slot, given that it has *already* done so five times in a row.

Imagine, for example, a simple game of luck where people compete with each other on the toss of a coin. In round one there are sixty-four people, round two thirty-two, round three sixteen and so on until in the final there are just two. At the start of the contest, the chances of any given person winning are 64–1. But by the time you get to the final, each remaining contestant has a 50–50 chance of winning. On Marge's logic, however, the odds are fixed at round one. And so, in the final, although there are only two people left, Marge would reason that each one has only a 1 in 64 chance of winning. Which would mean, of course, that that there is only a 1 in 32 chance of either person winning!

To return to the roulette wheel, it is indeed very unlikely that the ball will fall into the same colour slot six times in a row, just as it is very unlikely (64–1) that any given person will win the coin-tossing contest. But once the ball has fallen into the same colour slot five times, the initial improbability of a sequence of six is irrelevant: for the next spin of the wheel the chances of the ball falling into either red or black is a little less than 50–50 (there are also two green slots on the wheel).

The point is that the improbability of what has happened in the past does not affect the probability of what is yet to happen. Marge should have seen this. Had she observed how frequently a series of five of the same colour extended into a series of six, she would have seen that the chances were in fact, a little less than 50-50. Her mistake, then, was not just one of faulty reasoning, but of imagining something to be the case that her observations could have confirmed was not. She is a poor experimenter, in her head and the world.

See also

3. The Indian and the ice
16. Racing tortoises
42. Take the money and run
94. The Sorites tax

7. When no one wins

Private Sacks was about to do a terrible thing. He had been ordered to first rape and then murder the prisoner, whom he knew to be no more than an innocent civilian from the wrong ethnic background. There was no doubt in his mind that this would be a gross injustice – a war crime, in fact.

Yet quickly thinking it over he felt he had no choice but to go ahead. If he obeyed the order, he could make the ordeal as bearable as possible for the victim, making sure she suffered no more than was necessary. If he did not obey the order, he himself would be shot and the prisoner would still be violated and killed, but probably more violently. It was better for everyone if he went ahead.

His reasoning seemed clear enough, but of course it gave him no peace of mind. How could it be that he was both going to do the best he could in the circumstances and also a terrible wrong?

'If I don't do it somebody else will' is generally speaking a weak justification for wrongdoing. You are responsible for the wrong you do, regardless of whether or not others would have done it anyway. If you see an open-top sports car with the keys in the ignition, jump in and drive it away, your action does not stop being theft simply because it was only a matter of time before someone else did the same.

In Sacks's case, the justification is subtly different, and importantly so. For what he is saying is, 'If I don't do it somebody else will, with much worse consequences.' Sacks is not just resigned to the bad to come; he is trying to make sure the best possible – or least worst – thing happens.

Usually, it would seem perfectly moral to do what you can to prevent as much harm as possible. The best Sacks can do is save his own life and make the death of the prisoner as painless as possible. Yet this reasoning leads him to take part in a rape and murder, and surely that can never be the morally right thing to do.

The temptation to imagine a third possibility – perhaps just shooting the prisoner and himself – is hard to resist. But resist it we must, for in a thought experiment we control the variables, and what we are asking in this one is what he should do if the only two possibilities are to carry out the order or to refuse to do so. The whole point of fixing the dilemma this way is to force us to confront the moral problem head on, not think our way around it.

Some might argue that there are occasions when it is impossible to do the right thing. Damned if you do and damned if you don't, immorality is unavoidable. In such circumstances, we should pursue the least bad option. That allows us to say that Sacks both does the best he can and does wrong. But this solution merely creates a different problem. If Sacks did the best he can, then how could we blame him or punish him for what he did? And if he deserves no blame or punishment, surely he did no wrong?

Perhaps then the answer is that an action can be wrong, but the person doing it blameless. What he *did* was wrong but he was not wrong to do it. The logic holds. But does it reflect the complexity of the world or is it a sophistical contortion to justify the unjustifiable?

The alternative is to say that the end does not justify the means. Sacks should refuse. He will die and the prisoner suffer more, but it is the only moral choice available to him. That may preserve Sacks's integrity, but is that a nobler goal than the saving of lives and the relief of suffering?

See also

44. Till death us do part
55. Sustainable development
82. The freeloader
91. No one gets hurt

8. Good God

And the Lord spake unto the philosopher, 'I am the Lord thy God, and I am the source of all that is good. Why does thy secular moral philosophy ignore me?'

And the philosopher spake unto the Lord, 'To answer I must first ask you some questions. You command us to do what is good. But is it good because you command it, or do you command it because it is good?'

'Ur,' said the Lord. 'It's good because I command it?'

'The wrong answer, surely, your mightiness! If the good is only good because you say it is so, then you could, if you wished, make it so that torturing infants was good. But that would be absurd, wouldn't it?'

'Of course!' replieth the Lord. 'I tested thee and thou hast made me pleased. What was the other choice again?'

'You choose what is good because it *is* good. But that shows quite clearly that goodness does not depend on you at all. So we don't need to study God to study the good.'

'Even so,' spake the Lord, 'you've got to admit I've written some pretty good textbooks on the subject . . .'

Source: *Euthyphro* by Plato (380 BCE)

When I was at school, we used to sing a hymn in which God was equated with virtually every positive attribute. We sang that God is love, God is good, God is truth, and God is beauty. No wonder the chorus ended 'praise him!'.

The idea that God is good, however, is ambiguous. It could mean that God is good in the same way that cake is good, or Jo is good. In these cases, 'is' functions to attribute a quality or property to something, such as goodness or blueness. Equally, however, 'God is good' could be a sentence like 'Water is H_2O' or 'Plato is the author of *The Republic*'. Here, 'is' indicates an identity between the two terms: the one thing is identical to the other.

In the hymn, the 'is' seemed to be one of identity, not attribution. God is not loving but love; not beautiful but beauty. God doesn't just have these fine qualities, he *is* them. Hence 'God is good' implies that the notions of God and goodness are inextricably linked, that the essence of the good is God.

If this is so, then it is no wonder that many believe that there can be no morality without God. If goodness and Godness cannot be separated, secular morality is a contradiction in terms.

However, our imaginary conversation seems to demonstrate very clearly and simply that this cannot be so. If God is good, it is because God is and chooses to do what is *already* good. God doesn't make something good by choosing it; he chooses it because it is good.

Some might protest that this argument works only because it separates what cannot be separated. If God really is good, then it doesn't make sense to pose a dilemma in which the good and God are distinguished. But since it seems to make perfect sense to ask whether the good is good because God commands it, or God commands it because it is good, this objection simply begs the question.

Even if God and the good really were one, it would still be reasonable to ask what makes this identity true. The answer would surely be that we know what good is and it is this which would enable us to say truly that God is good. If God advocated pointless torture, we would know that he was not good. This shows that we can understand the nature of goodness independently of God. And that shows that a godless morality is not an oxymoron.

See also

17. The torture option
57. Eating Tiddles
58. Divine command
95. The problem of evil

9. Bigger Brother

For the seventy-third series of *Big Brother*, the producers had introduced a fiendish new toy: Pierre. The show's consultant psychologist explained how it would work.

'As you know, the brain is the engine of thought and action, and the brain is entirely physical. Our understanding of the laws of physics is such that we can now accurately predict how people's brains will react – and thus how people will think – in response to events in their environment.

'On entering the Big Brother space station, a brain scanner maps the brain states of all the participants. Our supercomputer, Pierre, monitors the various stimuli the contestants are exposed to and is able then to predict what their future behaviour will be.

'Of course, all this is so fiendishly complicated that there are severe limits. That is why the technology works best in a controlled, enclosed environment such as the Big Brother space station, and also why predictions can only be made for a few moments ahead, since tiny errors in predictions soon compound themselves into large ones. But viewers will enjoy seeing the computer predict how the contestants are about to react. In a sense, we will know their minds better than they do themselves.'

Source: The deterministic thesis of the French mathematician Pierre-Simon Laplace (1749–1827)

The French scientist Pierre Laplace suggested that if we knew both the laws of physics and the location of every particle in the universe, we would be able to predict everything that would come to pass in the future. Quantum theory has shown that to be false since not all causal processes are strictly determined by prior conditions. There is more indeterminacy in the universe than Laplace supposed.

Nevertheless, quantum effects occur only at the smallest level, and most objects in the world do work as though they were strictly determined by prior causes, just as Laplace thought. It therefore seems possible that we could adopt something less complete than the stance of Laplace's all-seeing observer and make more modest predictions. In short, the Big Brother computer is still a theoretical possibility.

It could be very unsettling to watch the show with the benefit of Pierre's predictions. We would see people behave time and time again exactly as predicted by a computer that had knowledge only of the physical states of their brains and environments. Contestants would be making decisions that the computer calculated they were bound to make. In short, they would appear not to be free agents making autonomous choices, but automata.

How should we respond to this prospect? One way is to deny its possibility. Human beings do have free will, and that means no computer could ever do what we imagine Pierre doing. However, this response looks like an example of simply refusing to accept what we don't like. We need to know why Pierre is not possible, not merely be told that it isn't.

The appeal to quantum indeterminacy won't do. Even if it is true that quantum theory introduces more unpredictability than our thought experiment has allowed, all it would do is replace an entirely predictable causal process with one which contains unpredictable, random elements. But our actions are no more free if they are the result of random causal processes than if they are the result of strictly determined ones. Free will appears to require that we escape the physical causal chain altogether. And that, it seems, we cannot do.

The second response is to accept that Pierre is possible, but argue that free will, in some important sense, is not threatened by it. One possible route is to drive a wedge between the notions of predictability and freedom. We can often predict, for example, what food or drink our friends will order, but we do not suppose that their choice is therefore not free. If that is true, why should we think that being able to predict *all* of a person's behaviour would show that they are not free?

But would that really save free will? What is freedom if not the ability to do what you choose, irrespective of what has happened up until the moment of the choice?

See also

36. Pre-emptive justice
39. The Chinese room
64. Nipping the bud
92. Autogovernment

10. The veil of ignorance

The twenty civilians selected to go and live on the Mars colony were set an unusual task. On the red planet there would be a number of goods, including accommodation, food, drink and luxury items. They had to decide, before they went out, on what basis those goods would be distributed. But, crucially, they did not know what the most important tasks would be on the colony. All the work could be manual, or none of it. It might require great intelligence, it might be better suited to those less in need of mental stimulation.

The first suggestion made was that everything should be shared equally: from each according to their abilities, to each according to their needs. But then someone raised an objection. If there was lots of work to be done and someone refused to do their share, wouldn't it be unfair to reward them with an equal slice of the cake? Surely there needed to be an incentive to contribute?

The objection was accepted, but that just seemed to lead to more problems. Fairness did not appear to mean the same as giving everyone the same. But what then did it mean?

Source: Chapter 3 of *A Theory of Justice* by John Rawls (Harvard University Press, 1971)

According to the political philosopher John Rawls, although the colonists do not yet know what fairness is, they are in the ideal position to find out. For they are making their decisions about the right way to distribute goods behind a 'veil of ignorance' that leaves them in the dark as to how easily they will cope with life on the colony. That means we can trust their decisions to be totally impartial. For example, since no one knows whether intellectual or physical work will be more valuable on Mars, the colonisers should not gamble on a system whereby either type of work is better remunerated. That would lead them to treat those with different skills the same, which seems to be very fair indeed.

Rawls thought that if we want to know what fairness is on Earth, we should imagine ourselves to be in a similar position. The key difference is that we should also imagine that we do not know whether we will be smart or stupid, dextrous or clumsy, fit or sickly. That way we will be able to come up with rules to determine how to distribute goods which are completely fair and do not discriminate against anyone.

Rawls thought that if we undertook this process rationally, we would end up with a system in which we always make sure the worst off are as well off as possible. This is because we would not know if we would ourselves be on society's scrapheap. Therefore we would prudently make sure that, if we were among the unfortunate, we would still have as much as possible. All this leads to a traditional form of liberal social democracy, in which some variations in fortune are allowed, just as long as it is not to the cost of the least fortunate.

Is this really fair or rational, though? How do we respond to the person who argues that there is nothing unfair in allowing the least capable to sink? Or what about the claim that it is perfectly rational to gamble on being one of life's winners rather than play safe and vote for a society in which the losers are protected as much as possible? Are we failing to be impartial if we take as our guiding principle what would happen to *us* in this society, rather than simply considering what is fair and just?

Fans of Rawls believe the veil of ignorance is the best device we have for deciding what a fair society would look like. Critics say that it does no such thing: when we go behind the veil we simply take our existing political views and prejudices and make our decisions accordingly. It can therefore be seen as either the most useful or useless thought experiment in the history of political philosophy.

See also

22. The lifeboat
29. Life dependency
87. Fair inequality
100. The Nest café

11. The ship *Theseus*

This is not what Ray North had bargained for. As an international master criminal he prided himself on being able to get the job done. His latest client had demanded that he steal the famous yacht *Theseus*, the vessel from which British newspaper magnate Lucas Grub had thrown himself to his death and which more recently had been the scene of the murder of LA rapper Daddy Iced Tea.

But here he was in the dry dock where the boat had just finished being repaired, confronted by two seemingly identical yachts. North turned to the security man, who was being held at gunpoint by one of his cronies.

'If you want to live, you'd better tell me which one of these is the real *Theseus*,' demanded Ray.

'That kinda depends,' came the nervous reply. 'You see, when we started to repair the ship, we needed to replace lots of parts. Only, we kept all the old parts. But as the work progressed, we ended up replacing virtually everything. When we had finished, some of the guys thought it would be good to use all the old parts to reconstruct another version of the ship. So that's what we've got. On the left, the *Theseus* repaired with new parts and on the right, the *Theseus* restored from old parts.'

'But which one is the genuine *Theseus*?' demanded Ray.

'I've told you all I know!' screamed the guard, as the crony tightened his grip. Ray scratched his head and started to think about how he could get away with both . . .

Source: *Leviathan* by Thomas Hobbes (1651)

Philosophy concerns itself with the questions that still remain unanswered once all the facts have been collected. In this scenario, Ray knows all the relevant facts about the two boats. Yet the answer to his question remains mysterious.

For some people, it is intuitively obvious which is the genuine *Theseus*. But which answer they give will depend on how you tell the story. If Ray were a detective looking to gather forensic evidence about the deaths of Lucas Grub and Daddy Iced Tea, it would seem pretty obvious that he would count the reconstructed *Theseus* as the genuine article. He might reach the same conclusion if he were a collector of objects with a historical significance.

However, if there were an ownership dispute, the repaired *Theseus* would be counted as the original. That is the boat the owner is entitled to sail away. And if you were to have placed a time-delay camera in the dry dock and followed the progress of the works, you would have seen the boat that came in gradually being worked on with the repaired version as the end result, while the restored one would have only later started to emerge beside it. The repaired ship thus has a continuity of existence which the restored one does not.

You might then think that which is the 'genuine' *Theseus* is not a question with a single answer. It all depends on what your interest in the boat is. But this answer may have disturbing consequences. For are not people rather like *Theseus*? As we go through life, the cells in our body continually die and are replaced. Our thoughts too change, so that little of what was in our heads when we were ten years old remains when we are twenty, and these thoughts, memories, convictions and dispositions are in turn replaced as we grow older. Are we then to say that there is no right answer as to whether we are the same people who we were many years ago and that it just depends on what our interest in ourselves is? If the identity of *Theseus* is not a factual matter, then can there be a fact about the identity of anything that gradually changes over time, human beings included?

See also

2. Beam me up . . .
46. Amoebaesque
65. Soul power
74. Water, water, everywhere

12. Picasso on the beach

Roy looked down from the cliffs at the man drawing in the sand. The picture that started to emerge startled him. It was an extraordinary face, not realistically rendered, but seemingly viewed from many angles at once. In fact, it looked much like a Picasso.

As soon as the thought entered his mind, his heart stopped. He lifted his binoculars to his eyes, which he then felt compelled to rub. The man on the beach *was* Picasso.

Roy's pulse raced. He walked this route every day, and he knew that very soon the tide would sweep in and wash away a genuine Picasso original. Somehow, he had to try and save it. But how?

Trying to hold back the sea was futile. Nor was there any way to take a cast of the sand, even if he had had the time he was actually so short of. Perhaps he could run back home for his camera. But that would at best preserve a record of the work, not the picture itself. And if he did try this, by the time he got back, the image would probably have been erased by the ocean. Perhaps then he should simply enjoy this private view as long as it lasted. As he stood watching, he didn't know whether to smile or cry.

Source: 'In a Season of Calm Weather' by Ray Bradbury, reprinted in *A Medicine for Melancholy* (Avon Books, 1981)

There is no general principle which states that there is something tragic about a work of art which doesn't persist over time. It depends entirely on what form the art takes. It is just absurd to think that a performance should have a permanent existence in the same way that a sculpture does. Of course, we can film a performance, or preserve its script. But neither of these methods freezes the work itself in time, as anyone who has seen a memorable play or concert and then watched it on film knows.

When it comes to sculpture and painting, preservation is seen as the ideal. But how sharp is the distinction between the performance and plastic arts? Picasso's imaginary sand sketch certainly blurs the boundaries. The unusual choice of medium means that that which usually endures is transformed into a fleeting performance.

Recognising that there is no sharp dividing line between the performative and the plastic may prompt us to reconsider our attitudes towards preservation and restoration. In general, we assume that it is desirable to keep, or restore, pictures so that they are as similar to how they were when they were new. But perhaps we should see the slow deterioration of artworks as an essential part of their performative dimension.

It is certainly the case that many artists take into account how their works will age when they create them. Frank Gehry, for example, knew how exposure to the elements would affect the titanium exterior of his architectural masterpiece, the Guggenheim museum in Bilbao. Similarly, the old masters were not ignorant about how their pigments would age.

Perhaps we could go further and say that our desire to preserve is a form of denial about our own mortality. The fact that art can endure longer than people has led some to seek a form of proxy immortality through it. (Although Woody Allen famously claimed he did not want immortality through art, but through not dying.) If we accept that art is mortal too, and that nothing is truly permanent, maybe we can see more clearly where the value of art and life is to be found: in experiencing them.

See also

37. Nature the artist
48. Evil genius
66. The forger
86. Art for art's sake

13. Black, white and red all over

Mary knows everything there is to know about the colour red. As a scientist, it has been her life's work. If you want to know why we can't see infrared, why tomatoes are red or why red is the colour of passion, Mary is your woman.

All this would be unremarkable, if it weren't for the fact that Mary is an achromat: she has no colour vision at all. The world, for Mary, looks like a black and white movie.

Now, however, all that is to change. The cones on her retina are not themselves defective, it is simply that the signals are not processed by the brain. Advances in neurosurgery now mean that this can be fixed. Mary will soon see the world in colour for the first time.

So despite her wide knowledge, perhaps she doesn't know everything about the colour red after all. There is one thing left for her to find out: what red looks like.

Source: 'What Mary Didn't Know' by Frank Jackson, republished in *The Nature of Mind*, edited by David Rosenthal (Oxford University Press, 1991)

Most educated people don't have much time for the view that mind and body are two different kinds of stuff, which somehow coexist side by side. The idea that we have an immaterial soul that inhabits our animal bodies – a ghost in the machine – is outmoded, implausible and anti-scientific.

Simply rejecting one erroneous worldview, however, does not guarantee you will be left with a true one. If you kick out mind–body dualism, what is to replace it? The obvious candidate is physicalism: there is only one kind of stuff, physical stuff, and everything, including the human mind, is made of it. For sure, this 'stuff' may turn out to be energy rather than little sub-atomic billiard balls, but whatever chairs are made of, everything else is made of too.

And so it may be. But physicalist zeal can go too far. Even if there is just one class of 'stuff', that doesn't necessarily mean the word can be understood in entirely physical terms.

This is what the story of Mary illustrates. As a scientist, Mary knows everything about red in *physical* terms. Yet there is something she doesn't know: what it *looks like*. No scientific account of the world can give her this knowledge. Science is objective, experimental, quantitative; sense experience – indeed all mental experience – is subjective, experiential and qualitative. What this seems to show is that no physical description of the world, however complete, can capture what goes on in our minds. As philosophers put it, the mental is irreducible to the physical.

This presents a challenge to physicalists. How can it be true both that there is nothing in the world apart from physical stuff, and yet the same time, that there are mental events that cannot be explained in physical terms? Is this a case of jumping out of the dualist frying pan into the physicalist fire?

Let us imagine that Mary is herself a physicalist. What might she say? Perhaps she would start by pointing out that there is a difference between appearances and reality: there is a way things are and a way they appear to be. Science concerns itself with the former, not the latter, because knowledge is always of how things are, not as they merely seem to be. Mary knows everything about what red is, she just doesn't 'know' how it appears to most people. She does know how it appears to her, of course, which is like a particular shade of grey.

So when Mary sees colour for the first time, the world will *appear* a new way for her. But is it true to say she will know anything new about it? It may seem natural to say she now 'knows' what red looks like. But sometimes our ordinary ways of talking can blind us to the subtler distinctions a philosopher should take care to make.

See also

21. Land of the Epiphens
41. Getting the blues
59. The eyes have it
73. Being a bat

14. Bank error in your favour

When Richard went to the ATM, he got a very pleasant surprise. He requested £100 with a receipt. What he got was £10,000 with a receipt – for £100.

When he got home, he checked his account online and found that, sure enough, his account had been debited by only £100. He put the money in a safe place, fully expecting the bank swiftly to spot the mistake and ask for it back. But the weeks passed and nobody called.

After two months, Richard concluded that no one was going to ask for the money. So he headed off to the BMW dealership with the hefty down-payment in his pocket.

On the way, however, he did feel a twinge of guilt. Wasn't this stealing? He quickly managed to convince himself it was no such thing. He had not deliberately taken the money, it had just been given to him. And he hadn't taken it from anyone else, so no one had been robbed. As for the bank, this was a drop in the ocean for them, and anyway, they would be insured against such eventualities. And it was their fault they had lost the money – they should have had safer systems. No, this wasn't theft. It was just the biggest stroke of luck he had ever had.

I don't know anyone who, on picking the 'bank error in your favour – collect £200' card in Monopoly, returns the cash to the bank on the grounds that it is not really theirs. In real life, however, we might expect an honest person to do just that. But how many people would? Not that many, I'd guess.

It is not that people are plain immoral. Indeed, we make quite fine discriminations in such cases. For instance, if people are accidentally given too much change by a small, independent business, they are more likely to point out the mistake than they are if it is made by a large corporation. The principle seems to be that it is wrong to take advantage of the mistakes of a fellow human being, but big businesses are fair game. This is probably in part because we sense that no one is really harmed by the error of a corporate entity, and the loss to them is insignificant compared to the benefit to us. In a strange way, then, our willingness to take the money is fuelled in part by a peculiar sense of justice.

But even if we do conclude that this is a form of justifiable theft, it is theft nonetheless. The fact that it is the result of an accident, with no intention to steal, is irrelevant. For example, imagine you mistakenly take someone else's bag at the luggage reclaim and subsequently find that it contains many more valuable items than were in your own. If you then make no efforts to return it, the accidental nature of the initial acquisition does not justify the later, very deliberate, decision not to do anything about it. Similarly, you would be rightly annoyed if someone took something of value which you had accidentally left unattended, reasoning that it was your fault for not being careful enough.

Richard's thought that the bank could well afford the loss is also spurious, for if that justifies his actions then it also justifies shoplifting. Shops are also insured and a small theft will barely dent their profits.

The reason why Richard was so easily persuaded by his own arguments is that, like all of us, he is prone to self-serving bias in his thinking. Reasons that justify benefits to ourselves seem more persuasive than those that don't. It is very difficult to disable this bias and think impartially. After all, why would we want to do that?

See also

7. When no one wins
82. The freeloader
83. The golden rule
91. No one gets hurt

15. Ordinary heroism

It came as a great surprise to his family that Private Kenny was not awarded the Victoria Cross for bravery. After all, he had died smothering a grenade that would have killed a dozen or more of his comrades. If that was not a 'signal act of valour or devotion in the presence of the enemy' then what was?

They demanded an explanation from his regiment. The statement issued by the army read: 'It has been the practice in the past to reward such actions with the appropriate medal. However, we have decided that it is a mistake to consider such acts as requiring an exceptional devotion to duty. All military personnel are required to act in the interests of the whole unit at all times. To suggest that Private Kenny's act was over and above the call of duty, therefore, suggests that it might be acceptable sometimes not to act in the interests of the whole unit. This is clearly absurd. Therefore, we no longer reward such acts with posthumous awards.

'Although we appreciate this is a painful time for the family, we should also point out that Private Kenny would have died in the blast anyway, so it is not even the case that he sacrificed his life for his colleagues.'

It was hard to fault the cold logic of the statement, but in their hearts Kenny's family were not persuaded that he had acted anything other than heroically. But on what grounds could they appeal?

Private Kenny's story seems to be an example of what philosophers call supererogatory behaviour. This is when someone does something good which goes beyond what is demanded of them by morality. So, for example, morality obliges you to pluck a drowning child out of a pond when it is not difficult to do so, but to leap into a stormy sea, risking your own life, to save someone is to do more than morality requires. To put it another way, someone will be praised for doing a supererogatory act, but won't be blamed for not doing it.

That there is a difference between things we are obliged to do and supererogatory acts seems to be a given. It is therefore considered a problem for any moral theory if it elides the difference. This seems to be the case with utilitarianism, which says that the morally right action is the one which benefits the greatest number. If this is true, then it seems we fail to do the right thing whenever we fail to do what is in the interests of the largest number of people, even if to do so would require great personal sacrifice. For instance, it could be argued that to live even a fairly modest western lifestyle while thousands die in poverty every hour is to fail to do what morality requires, since we could be saving lives and we choose not to. What is more, helping the poor needn't even require great sacrifice, relatively speaking, since we would have to give up only some comforts which are, in the grand scheme of things, luxuries.

However, when someone does dedicate their lives to helping the poor, we tend to think that they have gone beyond the call of duty, not simply done what morality requires. It could be, of course, that we like to think this because it gets us off the hook. After all, if morality required that we did the same, then we are moral failures. In the same way, any soldier who didn't act as Private Kenny did would have acted immorally. Kenny did only what any decent person should do in the circumstances: no more and no less.

Perhaps it is a purely intellectual exercise to worry about whether acts usually considered heroic are supererogatory or simply what morality requires. The fact remains that human nature being what it is, we all know that some acts require extraordinary efforts. Whether such people do more than morality demands or whether the majority of us are moral failures doesn't change that.

See also

29. Life dependency
53. Double trouble
71. Life support
89. Kill and let die

16. Racing tortoises

Welcome to the Great Athenian Man–Tortoise Run-off. My name's Zeno and I'll be your commentator for the big race. I have to say, however, that the result is a foregone conclusion. Achilles has made the terrible mistake of giving Tarquin the tortoise a 100-yard head start. Let me explain.

Tarquin's tactic is to keep constantly moving, however slowly. If Achilles is to overtake Tarquin, first he must get to where Tarquin is when the race starts. That will take him several seconds. In that time, Tarquin will have moved on a little and will then be a short distance ahead of Achilles. Now if Achilles is to overtake Tarquin, he must again get to where Tarquin is first. But in the time it takes Achilles to do that, Tarquin will again have moved forward slightly. So, Achilles once more needs to get to where Tarquin is now, in order to overtake him, in which time, Tarquin would have moved forward. And so on. You get the picture. It's just logically and mathematically impossible for Achilles to overtake the beast.

Still, it's too late to place your bets on the tortoise now, because they're under starter's orders, and . . . they're off! Achilles is closing . . . closing . . . closing . . . Achilles has overtaken the tortoise! I can't believe it! It's impossible!

Source: The ancient paradox of Achilles and the Tortoise, attributed to Zeno (born *c.* 488 BCE)

Zeno's explanation of why Achilles can't overtake the tortoise is a paradox, because it leads us to the conclusion that two incompatible things are true. The argument seems to demonstrate that Achilles can't overtake the tortoise, but experience tells us that of course he can. But there seems to be nothing wrong either with the argument or with what experience tells us.

Some have thought they can identify a flaw in the argument. It works only if you assume that time and space are continuous wholes which can be divided up into ever smaller chunks *ad infinitum*. This is because the argument depends on the idea that there is always a length of space, however small, over which the tortoise will have moved on a little distance, however short, in the period of time, however brief, it takes Achilles to get to where the tortoise was. Perhaps this assumption is just wrong. Eventually you reach a point in time and space that can't be carved up any smaller.

However, this in itself simply creates different paradoxes. The problem with this idea is that it claims the smallest unit of space essentially has no extension (length, height or width) because if it did, it would be possible to divide it up further and we'd be back with the problems of the race paradox. But then how can space, which clearly does have extension, be made up of units which do not themselves have extension? The same problem occurs with time. If the smallest unit of time has no duration and so cannot be divided any further, how can time as a whole have duration?

So we are left with a paradox of paradoxes: two paradoxes, both of which seem genuine, but which, if both are true, would make the only two possibilities impossible. Confused? Don't worry – you should be.

There is no simple way out. Solutions actually require quite complex mathematics. And this is perhaps the real lesson of the tortoise race: armchair theorising using basic logic is an unreliable guide to the fundamental nature of the universe. But that in itself is a sobering lesson, because we rely upon basic logic all the time to spot inconsistencies and flaws in argument. It is not logic itself which is at fault: the more complex solutions to paradoxes such as these themselves depend on holding the laws of logic firm. The difficulty is rather with applying it.

See also

6. Wheel of fortune
42. Take the money and run
70. An inspector calls
94. The Sorites tax

17. The torture option

Hadi's captives looked resolute, but he was sure he could break them, as long as he followed through on his threat. The father, Brad, was the real villain. It was he who had planted the huge bomb that he promised would kill hundreds, perhaps thousands, of innocent civilians. Only he knew where the bomb was, and he wasn't telling.

His son, Wesley, had nothing to do with it. But Hadi's intelligence told him that, though Brad would not break under torture, he almost certainly would if he were to see his son tortured in front of him. Not immediately, but soon enough.

Hadi was torn. He had always opposed torture and would probably have to leave the room while it was carried out. Wesley's innocence was not the only reason for his qualms, but it certainly exacerbated them. But he also knew this was the only way to save hundreds of people from death and mutilation. If he didn't order the torture, would he be condemning people to death, just because of his own squeamishness and lack of moral courage?

For many years scenarios such as this were considered to be purely hypothetical. Civilised societies did not permit torture. All that changed with the 'war on terror', and in particular the scandal surrounding the treatment of prisoners at Abu Ghraib prison in Iraq. The argument was not just about whether the bad treatment had taken place and, if so, who had authorised it; but about whether it was necessarily wrong.

Hadi's dilemma is a simplified version of a situation it is surely possible for moral, responsible persons to be placed in. Defenders of torture under such circumstances would say that, terrible though it may be, you have little choice but to go ahead. For example, how could you risk another 9-11 by refusing to torture one person, or a few people? Isn't that a kind of moral self-indulgence? You keep yourself pure by not doing the dirty deeds necessary, but at the cost of innocent lives. And if you can see the case for Hadi ordering the torture of Wesley – who is, after all, innocent – then the case for torturing the guilty is even stronger.

The argument is a challenging one for defenders of human rights, who have tended to see all torture as indefensible. To maintain their position, they can adopt one of two strategies. The first is to insist that the torture is in principle wrong. Even if it would save thousands of lives, there are some moral lines that cannot be crossed. There is an arguable case for this position, but the charge of indifference to the lives of those left to die as a result is hard to shake.

The other strategy is to argue that, although in theory torture may sometimes be morally acceptable in rare cases, we need to maintain an absolute prohibition against it in order to hold the moral line. In practice, if torture is sometimes allowed, it will inevitably go on when it should not. It is better that we sometimes fail to torture when it is the best thing to do than occasionally torture when it is wrong to do so.

This argument, however, may not help Hadi. For, though there may be good reasons to adopt a rule that there should be no torture, Hadi is faced with a specific situation where the benefits of torture are clear. The dilemma he has is not whether torture should be permitted, but whether on this occasion he should break the rules and do what is not permitted, in order to save innocent lives. You may well think that he should not do so, but surely it is clear that his choice is not an easy one.

See also

18. Rationality demands
50. The good bribe
57. Eating Tiddles
79. A Clockwork Orange

18. Rationality demands

Sophia Maximus has always prided herself on her rationality. She would never knowingly act contrary to the dictates of reason. Of course, she understands that some of the basic motivations to action are not rational – such as love, taste and character. But not being rational is not the same as being irrational. It is neither rational nor irrational to prefer strawberries to raspberries. But, given that preference, it is irrational to buy raspberries when strawberries are just as cheap.

Right now, however, she is in something of a fix. A very intelligent friend has persuaded her that it would be perfectly rational to set off a bomb which will kill many innocent people without any obvious benefit, such as saving other lives. She feels sure that there must be something wrong with her friend's argument. But rationally, she cannot see it. What is worse, the argument suggests she should set off the bomb as soon as possible, so thinking longer is not an option.

In the past she has always thought it wrong to reject good rational arguments in favour of hunches or intuitions. Yet if she follows reason in this case, she can't help but feel she will be doing a terrible wrong. Should she knowingly follow the less rational path, or trust reason over feeling and detonate the bomb?

The lack of detail in this thought experiment may create some suspicion as to its validity. We are not told what this fiendish rational argument is that concludes it would be good to bomb innocent people. This vagueness is not really a problem, however. We know from experience that people have been convinced by rational arguments to do terrible things. In Stalin's Russia and Mao's China, for example, people were persuaded that it was for the best to denounce innocent friends. Those who oppose the use of the A-Bomb on Hiroshima and Nagasaki will also accept that those who made the decision did so, for the most part, on the basis of reasons they thought were compelling.

But, it will objected, weren't the rational arguments given in each of these cases flawed? If we could see the argument that perplexed Sophia, we would surely be able to show that there is something wrong with it. This, however, assumes there must be something wrong with the argument. If you believe that reason always demands what is right, then it may just be that, contrary to appearances, the bombing is right, not that the argument is wrong. To assume the argument is wrong is already to elevate an intuitive conviction over the dictates of reason.

In any case, the optimism that the rational always aligns with the good is misplaced. The problem with psychopaths, it is said, is not that they lack reason but feeling. The eighteenth-century Scottish philosopher David Hume would agree. He wrote, 'Reason is, and ought only to be, the slave of the passions.' If reason is isolated from feeling, we should not assume that it will always lead us to good.

Even if this view is too pessimistic and it is never rational to do evil, the problem we still face is that we can never be sure we are being perfectly rational. To those who saw the reason in Stalinism and Maoism, the logic did not seem flawed at all. Sophia is bright, but how can she tell whether reason really does demand she place the bomb or whether she has simply failed to spot the flaw in the argument? It is one thing to believe in the sovereignty of reason. It is quite another to believe in the power of human beings always to be able to recognise what that sovereign demands.

See also

7. When no one wins
44. Till death us do part
83. The golden rule
91. No one gets hurt

19. Bursting the soap bubble

Members of the bizarre Weatherfield sect lived a very secluded life at St Hilda Hogden House. All but the leader were forbidden any contact with the outside world and were taught that reality was the world portrayed in soap operas – the only television programmes they were allowed to watch. For the Weatherfieldians, as they were known, *Coronation Street, The Bold and the Beautiful, EastEnders* and *Neighbours* were not works of fiction but fly-on-the-wall documentaries. And since most of the members had been born in the commune, the pretence was not hard to maintain.

One day, however, disciple Kenneth, who had always been a touch rebellious, decided to leave Hogden's and visit the places he had seen so often on the altar box. This was, of course, strictly prohibited. But Kenneth managed to escape.

What he found amazed him. The biggest shock came when he managed to get to Coronation Street and discovered it wasn't in Weatherfield at all, but was a set in the Granada Studios.

But when he furtively returned to Hogden's and told his fellow disciples what he had discovered, he was dismissed as a lunatic. 'You should never have left,' they told him. 'It's not safe out there. The mind plays tricks on you!' And with that they chased him from the commune and forbade him to enter again.

Source: The allegory of the cave in *The Republic* by Plato (360 BCE)

The story of the Weatherfieldians is clearly an allegory. But what do its various elements represent?

There are many ways of translating the parable. There are some who claim that the world of ordinary experience is an illusion, and that the doors to the real world are opened by sacred drugs or practices of meditation. People who claim to have seen the truth this way are usually dismissed as dope-heads or wackos; but they think it is we who are the fools, trapped as we are within the limited world of sense experience.

More prosaically, the real-life Weatherfieldians are those who don't question what they are told, and simply accept everything that life presents them at face value. They may not literally believe that soap operas are true, but they do accept uncritically received wisdom, what they read in the papers and watch on the television. What exactly this is depends on how they have been socialised. So, for example, some people think it crazy to believe that the President of the United States could be guilty of terrorism. Others think it equally mad to maintain that, actually, he's quite a smart guy.

This raises the question of what the real-world counterpart of St Hilda Hogden House is. We do not generally isolate ourselves with bricks and mortar, but we do confine the ranges of our experience in many subtler ways. If you only ever read one newspaper, you are severely limiting the intellectual space which you inhabit. If you only ever discuss politics with people who share your broad opinions, you are erecting another metaphorical fence around your own little world. If you never try to see the world from another's point of view, let alone walk a mile in their bare feet, you are again refusing to look beyond the walls of the small, comfortable world you have constructed for yourself.

Perhaps the greatest difficulty we face in this regard is spotting the Kenneth within. How do we distinguish between the deluded fools who have mad worldviews and those who have genuinely discovered an unseen dimension of life that has eluded us? We can't give everyone who believes they have accessed hidden truths the benefit of the doubt. For one thing, since they all claim contradictory things, they can't all be right. But if we dismiss them all too readily, we risk being like the naive, foolish Weatherfieldians, fated to accept a life of illusion instead of one of reality.

See also

1. The evil demon
49. The hole in the sum of the parts
51. Living in a vat
61. Mozzarella moon

20. Condemned to life

Vitalia had discovered the secret of eternal life. Now she vowed to destroy it.

Two hundred years ago, she had been given the formula for an elixir of immortality by a certain Dr Makropulos. Young and foolish, she had prepared and drunk it. Now she cursed her greed for life. Friends, lovers and relatives had grown old and died, leaving her alone. With no death pursuing her, she lacked all drive and ambition, and all the projects she started seemed pointless. She had grown bored and weary, and now just longed for the grave.

Indeed, the quest for extinction had been the one goal which had given some shape and purpose to her life over the last half century. Now she finally had the antidote to the elixir. She had taken it a few days ago and could feel herself rapidly weakening. All that remained now was for her to make sure that no one else was condemned to life as she had been. The elixir itself had long been destroyed. Now, she took the piece of paper that specified the formula and tossed it into the fire. As she watched it burn, for the first time in decades, she smiled.

Source: 'The Makropulos Case', in *Problems of the Self* by Bernard Williams (Cambridge University Press, 1973)

The tragedy of human life, it is often thought, is that our mortality means that death is the only thing that we know for sure awaits us. The story of Vitalia turns this conventional wisdom on its head and suggests that immortality would be a curse. We need death to give shape and meaning to life. Without it, we would find life pointless. On this view, if hell is eternal damnation, the eternity of life in Hades would be enough to make it a place of punishment.

It is surprising how few people who think eternal life would be desirable think hard about what it would entail. That is understandable. What we primarily want is simply more life. The exact duration of the extra lease is not our prime concern. It does seem that seventy years, if we're lucky, isn't long enough. There are so many places to see, so much to do and experience. If only we had more time to do it!

But perhaps we cut our life plans to fit their expected duration, and so, however many years we had, we would still think they were not quite enough. Consider, for example, the phenomenon of 'middle youth'. A few generations ago, the vast majority would marry and have children in their twenties, or sooner. Now, with more money and the assumptions that we will live longer and can have children later, more and more people are enjoying a kind of extended adolescence, well into their thirties. Compared to every other previous generation, the reasonably affluent middle-youthers get to travel and experience much more. But are they satisfied? If anything, this generation dwells more than any before on what it doesn't have.

However much life we have, it never seems quite enough. Yet we are not so hungry that we make full use of the time we do have. And if we had endless time, the concept of 'making full use' would become meaningless. There would be no such thing as time wasted, because time would be in infinite supply. And without any reason to make the most of the life we have, wouldn't existence become a tedious, pointless burden?

Perhaps we deceive ourselves when we say that the shortness

of life is the problem. Since we cannot alter the duration of our lives, any tragedy that results from its brevity is not our fault. It is harder to admit that we are responsible for how we use the time allocated to us. Perhaps we should stop thinking 'if only I had more time' and think instead 'if only I made better use of the time I've got'.

See also

19. Bursting the soap bubble
52. More or less
69. The horror
97. Moral luck

21. Land of the Epiphens

Epiphenia was a remarkable planet. So like Earth in appearance, and yet its inhabitants were different in one remarkable way.

As one of them, Huxley, explained to the visiting Earthling Dirk, the Epiphens had long ago 'discovered' that their thoughts did not affect their actions. Thoughts were the effects of bodily processes, not the other way around. Dirk found this baffling.

'You can't really believe this,' he protested to Huxley. 'For instance, when we met in this bar, you said, "Gee, I could kill for a beer," and ordered one. Are you saying that the thought "I want a beer" had no effect on your actions?'

'Of course it didn't,' replied Huxley, as though the question were idiotic. 'We have thoughts and these often precede actions. But we know full well that these thoughts aren't *causing* the actions. My body and brain were already gearing up to order a beer. The thought "I could kill a beer" was just something that popped into my head as a result of what was happening in the physical brain and body. Thoughts don't cause actions.'

'For Epiphens, maybe,' replied Dirk.

'Well I can't see what's different about humans,' said Huxley, and for a while at least, nor could Dirk.

Source: Although he didn't use the term, 'epiphenomenalism' was championed by T. H. Huxley, notably in an 1874 paper called 'On the Hypothesis that Animals are Automata, and its History', republished in *Method and Results: Essays by Thomas H. Huxley* (D. Appleton and Company, 1898).

The American philosopher Jerry Fodor once said that if epiphenomenalism were true, it would be the end of the world. Epiphenomenalism is the view that thoughts and other mental events do not cause anything in the physical world, including our actions. Rather, the brain and the body work like some kind of purely physical machine, and our conscious experience is a by-product, caused by the machine but not affecting it.

The reason why this would be the end of the world is that everything we seem to believe about what we are apparently depends on the idea that thoughts do cause actions. If what goes on in our minds has no impact on what we actually do, the world as we think of it is just an illusion.

But is this really the consequence of accepting epiphenomenalism? The imaginary land of Epiphenia is designed to test the idea that no one can live with the truth of epiphenomenalism. The suggestion is that people could come to see epiphenomenalism as some banal truth which does not affect the way they live their lives. The crucial point is that how it feels to be an Epiphen is exactly the same as what it feels like to be a human being. In both cases, thought accompanies action in just the same way. The only difference is that Epiphens do not believe their thoughts are doing any causing.

Is it really possible, however, to divorce what we believe about the link between thought and action and how we actually live? People such as Fodor think not, but it is far from obvious why this separation can't be achieved. For example, take a situation where the thinking does seem to be crucial. Let's say you're trying to work out a solution to a tricky logical or mathematical problem. Eventually, the eureka moment comes. In this case, surely the actual thinking has to play a part in the explanation for your actions?

Well, no. Why can't I believe that the conscious experience

of thinking is just a byproduct of the computing that is going on at brain level? It may be the *necessary* byproduct. But just as the noise that a boiling pot of water makes is an inevitable byproduct of the heating without that meaning it is the noise which cooks the egg, so thought could be the necessary byproduct of neural computation that doesn't itself produce the solution to the problem.

Indeed, if you think about thinking, there does seem to be something almost involuntary about it. Solutions 'come to us', for example, not we to them. Reflect on what it really feels like to think, and the idea that it is a byproduct of a process you are not conscious of may not seem quite so fanciful.

See also

9. Bigger Brother
54. The elusive I
62. I think, therefore?
68. Mad pain

22. The lifeboat

'Right,' said Roger, the self-appointed captain of the lifeboat. 'There are twelve of us on this vessel, which is great, because it can hold up to twenty. And we have plenty of rations to last until someone comes to get us, which won't be longer than twenty-four hours. So, I think that means we can safely allow ourselves an extra chocolate biscuit and a shot of rum each. Any objections?'

'Much as I'd doubtless enjoy the extra biscuit,' said Mr Mates, 'shouldn't our main priority right now be to get the boat over there and pick up the poor drowning woman who has been shouting at us for the last half hour?' A few people looked down into the hull of the boat, embarrassed, while others shook their heads in disbelief.

'I thought we had agreed,' said Roger. 'It's not our fault she's drowning, and if we pick her up, we won't be able to enjoy our extra rations. Why should we disrupt our cosy set-up here?' There were grunts of agreement.

'Because we could save her, and if we don't she'll die. Isn't that reason enough?'

'Life's a bitch,' replied Roger. 'If she dies, it's not because we killed her. Anyone for a digestive?'

Source: 'Lifeboat Earth' by Onora O'Neill, republished in *World Hunger and Moral Obligation*, edited by W. Aiken and H. La Follette (Prentice-Hall, 1977)

The lifeboat metaphor is pretty easy to translate. The boat is the affluent West and the drowning woman those dying of malnutrition and preventable disease in the developing world. And the attitude of the developed world is, on this view, as callous as Roger's. We have enough food and medicine for everyone, but we would rather enjoy luxuries and let others die than forfeit our 'extra biscuit' and save them. If the people on the lifeboat are grossly immoral, then so are we.

The immorality is even more striking in another version of the analogy, in which the lifeboat represents the whole of the planet Earth and some people refuse to distribute the food to others already on board. If it seems cruel not to make the effort to get another person on to the boat, it seems even crueller to deny supplies to those already plucked from the water.

The image is powerful and the message shocking. But does the analogy stand up? Some might say the lifeboat scenario neglects the importance of property rights. Goods are placed on a lifeboat for those who need them, and nobody has a greater claim to them than anyone else. So we start from the assumption that anything other than an equal distribution according to need is unfair unless proven otherwise.

In the real world, however, food and other goods are not just sitting there waiting to be distributed. Wealth is created and earned. So if I refuse to give some of my surplus to someone else, I am not unfairly appropriating what is due to him, I am simply keeping what is rightfully mine.

However, even if the analogy is altered to reflect this fact, the apparent immorality does not disappear. Let us imagine that all the food and supplies on the boat belong to the individuals in it. Nevertheless, once in the boat, and once the need of the drowning woman is recognised, wouldn't it still be wrong to say, 'Let her die. These biscuits are mine!'? As long as there is enough surplus to provide for her too, the fact that she is dying should make us give up some of our privately owned provisions for her.

The UN has set a target for developed countries to give 0.7 per cent of their GDP to overseas aid. Few have met it. For the vast majority of people, to give even 1 per cent of their income to help the impoverished would have a negligible effect on their quality of life. The lifeboat analogy suggests that it is not so much that we would be good people if we did so, but that we are terribly wrong not to.

See also

10. The veil of ignorance
55. Sustainable development
87. Fair inequality
100. The Nest café

23. The beetle in the box

Ludwig and Bertie were two precocious little tykes. Like many children, they played games with their own private languages. One of their favourites, which mystified the adults around them, was called 'Beetle'.

It started one day when they found two boxes. Ludwig proposed that they took one each, and that each would only ever look inside his own box, not that of the other. What is more, he would never describe what was in his box or compare it to anything outside the box. Rather, each would simply name the contents of his box 'beetle'.

For some reason, this amused them greatly. Each would proudly say that he had a beetle in his box, but whenever someone asked them to explain what this beetle was, they refused. For all anyone knew, either or both boxes were empty, or each contained very different things. Nonetheless, they insisted on using the word 'beetle' to refer to the contents of their boxes and acted as though the word had a perfectly reasonable use in their game. This was unsettling, especially for grown ups. Was 'beetle' a nonsense word or did it have a private meaning that only the boys knew?

Source: *Philosophical Investigations* by Ludwig Wittgenstein (Blackwell, 1953)

This odd little game is a variation on one outlined by the maverick Austrian philosopher Ludwig Wittgenstein. For Wittgenstein, however, all language use is a kind of game, in that it relies upon a combination of rules and conventions, not all of which can be explicitly stated, and which only players of the game really understand.

The question Wittgenstein invites us to ask is: does the word 'beetle' refer to anything? And if it doesn't, what does it mean? Although the passage in which he discusses the beetle has endless interpretations, it seems clear that Wittgenstein believes that what is in the box makes no difference to how the word is used. So whatever the word means, if anything, the actual contents of the box have nothing to do with it.

That much seems clear. But why does this matter? After all, unlike Ludwig and Bertie, we don't play such eccentric games, do we? Perhaps we do. Consider what happens when I say, 'I have a pain in my knee.' The box in this case is my inner experience. As with Ludwig and Bertie's containers, no one else can look inside it; only I can. Nor can I describe it in terms of anything that is outside of myself. All the vocabulary of pain refers to sensations, and all of these are inside the boxes of our own subjective experience.

Nevertheless, you also have your 'box'. You also use the word 'pain' to refer to something that goes on inside it. And I can't see inside your experience either. So we appear to be in a situation remarkably similar to that of Bertie and Ludwig. We both have words that refer to things that only we can experience. But nevertheless, we go on using these words as though they were meaningful.

The lesson of the beetle example is that whatever is actually going on inside us has nothing to do with what a word like 'pain' means. This is highly counter-intuitive, since we assume that by 'pain' we mean some kind of private sensation. But the beetle argument seems to show that it *cannot* mean that. Rather, the rules that govern the correct use of 'pain', and thus also its meaning, are public. For all we know, when we both say we are feeling pain what is going on inside me is quite different from what goes on inside you. All that matters is that we both use it in situations where certain patterns of behaviour, such as grimacing and distraction, are evident. If that line of reasoning is correct, then our ordinary use of language is very close to the strange game of Ludwig and Bertie.

See also

47. Rabbit!
68. Mad pain
74. Water, water, everywhere
85. The nowhere man

24. Squaring the circle

And the Lord spake unto the philosopher, 'I am the Lord thy God, and I am all-powerful. There is nothing that you can say that can't be done. It's easy!'

And the philosopher spake unto the Lord, 'OK, your mightiness. Turn everything that is blue red and everything that is red blue.'

The Lord spake, 'Let there be colour inversion!' And there was colour inversion, much to the confusion of the flag-bearers of Poland and San Marino.

And the philosopher then spake unto the Lord, 'You want to impress me: make a square circle.'

The Lord spake, 'Let there be a square circle.' And there was.

But the philosopher protesteth, 'That's not a square circle. It's a square.'

The Lord grew angry. 'If I say it's a circle, it's a circle. Watch your impertinence or else I shall smite thee very roughly indeed.'

But the philosopher insisteth, 'I didn't ask you to change the meaning of the word "circle" so it just means "square". I wanted a genuinely square circle. Admit it – that's one thing you can't do.'

The Lord thought a short while, and then decided to answer by unleashing his mighty vengeance on the philosopher's smart little arse.

Lest there be any suspicion that God's alleged inability to create a square circle is simply a piece of atheist mockery, it should be pointed out that classic theists, such as St Thomas Aquinas, happily accepted such constraints on God's power. This might seem odd, since, if God is all-powerful, surely there is literally nothing he can't do?

Aquinas and the vast majority of his successors disagreed. They had little choice. Like most believers, Aquinas thought that belief in God was consistent with rationality. That is not to say that rationality provides all the sufficient reasons to believe in God, or that by applying rationality we can exhaust all there is to say about the divine. The more modest claim is that there is no conflict between rationality and belief in God. You don't have to be irrational to believe in God, even if it helps.

That means that any beliefs we hold about God must not be irrational. That means we cannot attribute any qualities to God which commit us to accepting irrational beliefs.

The problem with things such as square circles is that they are logically impossible. Since a circle is by definition a one-sided shape and a square a four-sided one, and a four-sided one-sided shape is a contradiction in terms, then a square circle is a contradiction in terms and impossible in all possible worlds. This much rationality demands. So if we are to say that God's omnipotence means he can create shapes such as square circles, then we wave goodbye to rationality.

For that reason most religious believers are happy to conclude that God's omnipotence means that he can do all that is logically possible, but not that which is logically impossible. This, they claim, is not a limit on God's power, since the idea of a being with more power collapses into contradiction.

If we accept this concession, however, the door opens to rational scrutiny of the concept of God and the coherence of belief in him. By accepting that belief in God must be in harmony with reason, the religious believer is obliged to take seriously claims that belief in God is irrational. Such arguments include the claim that God's supposed all-loving nature is incompatible with the unnecessary suffering we see in the world; or that divine punishment is immoral given that God is ultimately responsible for human nature. It is not good enough to say these are simply matters of faith, if you accept the requirement for faith to be compatible with reason.

The alternative route for believers is even more unpalatable: deny that reason has anything to do with it and bank solely on faith instead. What appears contrary to reason is thus dismissed as simply a divine mystery. Such a route is open to us, but to abandon reason so readily in one sphere of life while living as a reasonable person the rest of the time is arguably to live a divided life.

See also

8. Good God
45. The invisible gardener
73. Being a bat
95. The problem of evil

25. Buridan's an ass

Buridan was very hungry indeed. It had all started with his resolution that every decision he made should be completely rational. The problem was that he had run out of food, but lived equidistant between two identical branches of the Kwik-E-Mart. Since he had no more reason to go to one rather than the other, he was caught in a state of perpetual suspension, unable to find any rational grounds for choosing either supermarket.

As his stomach rumbling grew intolerable, he thought he had hit upon a solution. Since it was clearly irrational to starve himself to death, wouldn't it be rational to make a random choice between the two Kwik-E-Marts? He should simply toss a coin, or see which direction he felt like heading off in. That was surely more rational than sitting at home and doing nothing.

But would this course of action require him to break his rule about only making decisions that were completely rational? What his argument seemed to suggest is that it would be rational of him to make an irrational decision – such as one based on the toss of a coin. But is rational irrationality rational at all? Buridan's plummeting blood sugar level made the question impossible to answer.

Source: The paradox of Buridan's Ass, first discussed in the Middle Ages

Nothing confers the illusion of profundity more effectively than a wise-sounding paradox. How about, 'To move forwards, one must step back'? Try making up your own. It's easy to do. First, think of something you want to illuminate (knowledge, power, cats). Second, think of its opposite (ignorance, impotence, dogs). Finally, try to combine the two elements to suggest something wise. 'The highest knowledge is knowledge of ignorance.' 'Only the impotent know true power.' 'To know the cat, know also the dog.' Well, it usually works.

Buridan seems to have thought his way to something that sounds equally paradoxical: sometimes it is rational to do something irrational. Is this as empty as the injunction to know both cats and dogs, a genuine insight, or just plain incoherent?

It might be thought that it can never be rational to do something irrational. Consider, for example, if the supposedly irrational thing is to make a decision on the toss of a coin. If we say it is rational to do this, what we must be saying is that making the decision on the toss of a coin is rational after all, not that it is an irrational act we are rational to perform.

The apparent paradox is a result of a sloppiness of language. Tossing a coin is not necessarily an *irrational* way to make a decision, it is simply a *non-rational* one. That is to say, it is neither rational nor irrational, but a process into which rationality does not enter. Much of what we do is non-rational in this way. For example, if you prefer red wine to white, that is not irrational, but nor is it rational. The preference is not based on reasons at all, but on tastes.

Once we accept this, the paradox disappears. Buridan's conclusion is that it is sometimes rational to adopt non-rational procedures for decision-making. In his case, since reason cannot determine which supermarket he should visit, but he needs to visit one, it is perfectly reasonable to make a random selection. No paradox there.

The moral of the story is, however, extremely important. Many people argue that rationality is overrated, because not everything we do can be explained or determined rationally. This is to use the right reasons to reach the wrong conclusion. Rationality remains sovereign because only reason can tell us when we should adopt rational or non-rational procedures. For example, if a herbal medicine works, then rationality may tell us we should take it, even if we cannot rationally explain how it works. But rationality would caution against taking homeopathic medicines, since there are no reasons to think they are effective. Accepting that it can be rational to be non-rational does not open the door to irrationality.

See also

6. Wheel of fortune
16. Racing tortoises
42. Take the money and run
94. The Sorites tax

26. Pain's remains

The tension in the auditorium was palpable as the doctor donned his mask and gloves and prepared to take his needle and thread to the conscious patient's strapped-down leg. As he pushed the needle through the flesh, the patient let out an almighty cry of pain. But once the needle had passed through, he seemed unnaturally calm.

'How was that?' asked the doctor.

'Fine,' replied the patient, to gasps from the audience. 'It's just as you said, I remember you putting the needle through me, but I don't remember any pain.'

'So do you have any objection if I do the next stitch?'

'Not at all. I'm not at all apprehensive.'

The doctor turned to the audience and explained: 'The process I have developed does not, like an anaesthetic, remove the sensation of pain. What it does is prevent any memory of the pain being laid down in the patient's nervous system. If you are not going to remember your momentary pain, why fear it? Our patient here shows this is not just theoretical sophistry. You witnessed his pain, but he, having forgotten it, has no fear of repeating the experience. This enables us to conduct surgery with the patient fully conscious, which in some instances is extremely useful. Now if you'll excuse me, I have some more stitching to do.'

Political philosopher Jeremy Bentham argued that when thinking about the moral rights of animals, 'the question is not, "Can they reason?" nor, "Can they talk?" but rather, "Can they suffer?"' But what is it to suffer? It is often assumed that it is just to feel pain. So if animals can feel pain, they deserve moral consideration. That is because to feel pain is bad in itself, and so to cause any unnecessary pain is to increase the sum total of bad things for no good reason.

It does seem unarguable that pain is indeed a bad thing. But how bad *is* it? This thought experiment challenges the intuition that pain in itself is a very bad thing; it separates the sensation of pain from the anticipation and memory of pain. Our patient, because he does not remember his pain, does not have anything bad to associate with his imminent pain, and thus does not fear it either. Nevertheless, at the moment of feeling the pain, it is intense and very real.

Although it would still seem wrong to inflict any pain on the man for no reason at all, since at the moment of its infliction something unnecessarily bad would be going on, it does seem that causing such a pain is not a terrible wrongdoing. This is not least because the person feeling the pain neither fears nor remembers it.

What makes causing pain usually so wrong, then, must be something to do with the way in which it scars us in the longer run and creates fear. Perhaps this is how we should understand suffering. For example, a sharp, momentary pain in a tooth is unpleasant, but it passes and doesn't affect our lives much. But if you have such a pain regularly, you really do suffer. It is not so much that the pains add up. Rather, the repetition of the pain, the knowledge that it is to come again and the way in way each pain leaves a trace in the memory and colours the past with its negativity: all these factors link the individual instances of pain into a connected ongoing pattern which constitutes suffering.

If this is right, to answer Bentham's question about animals we need to know not only whether animals feel pain, but whether they have the memory and anticipation of pain that is necessary to suffering. Many animals surely do. A dog that is constantly mistreated does seem to be suffering. But less complex animals that live only in the moment arguably cannot suffer in that way. Could it be that a fish, for example, hanging from a rod, is not really suffering a slow and painful death, but is merely experiencing a series of disconnected painful moments? If so then, like our doctor, we may not feel there is anything terribly wrong about inflicting these fleeting pains.

See also

5. The pig that wants to be eaten
17. The torture option
57. Eating Tiddles
68. Mad pain

27. Duties done

Hew, Drew, Lou and Sue all promised their mother they would regularly write and let her know how they were getting on during their round-the-world trip.

Hew wrote his letters, but gave them to other people to post, none of whom bothered. So his mother never received any letters from him.

Drew wrote her letters and posted them herself, but she carelessly put them in disused boxes, attached too few stamps and made other mistakes which meant none of them ever arrived.

Lou wrote and posted all her letters properly, but the postal system let her down every time. Mother didn't hear from her.

Sue wrote and posted all her letters properly, and made brief phone calls to check they had arrived. Alas, none did.

Did any of the children keep their promise to their mother?

Source: The moral philosophy of H. A. Prichard, as critiqued by Mary Warnock in *What Philosophers Think*, edited by J. Baggini and J. Stangroom (Continuum, 2003)

A pressing ethical conundrum indeed! Such were the kinds of issues discussed for much of the twentieth century in British moral philosophy, before the radicalisation of the late 1960s brought a belated focus on issues of war, poverty and animal rights.

However, it would be foolish to dismiss problems like this out of hand. The context may be mundane, but the issue in moral theory it addresses is important. Do not be misled by the genteel scenario. The question is: at what point can we say we have discharged our moral responsibilities? It applies not only to sending news to parents, but to cancelling orders for nuclear attack.

The issue at stake is whether we can be said to have fulfilled our duty if the consequence we intend for our action does not come about. In general, it would seem to be too harsh a rule to say that the answer is always no. Sue did everything she could to ensure her letters got home, yet still they did not. How can she be responsible for that failure when it was not in her power to do any more? That is why we don't hold people responsible for failures if they did the best they could.

However, that does not mean that we excuse people when they make an insufficient effort. Both Hew and Drew seem not to have paid enough attention to their correspondence duties. Both could reasonably be said to have not fulfilled their promises.

Lou is the most interesting case, since she could have done more to ensure the news was getting there, but at the same time she seems to have done all that could reasonably be expected.

The idea of what is reasonable to expect is crucial here. If we were talking about an order to cancel a nuclear attack, then our expectation of the checks and extra measures that should be taken would be much higher. The extent to which we are required to make sure the desired outcome actually happens thus varies according to the seriousness of the outcome. It's OK to just forget to set the video recorder. Just forgetting to call off the troops is inexcusable.

The problem of the holiday letter touches on one of the most fundamental issues in moral philosophy: the link between agents, actions and their consequences. What this thought experiment suggests is that ethical reasoning cannot focus on just one of these aspects. If ethics is all about consequences, then we have the absurdity that even someone like Sue, who does all she can, still does wrong if her actions do not turn out right. If ethics does not concern itself with consequences at all, however, we have a different absurdity, for how can it *not* matter what actually happens as the result of our actions?

If the specific letter-posting problem is itself trivial, the issues it touches on certainly are not.

See also

4. A byte on the side
43. Future shock
96. Family first
97. Moral luck

28. The nightmare scenario

Lucy was having the most awful nightmare. She was dreaming that wolf-like monsters had burst through the windows in her bedroom while she was asleep and then started to tear her apart. She fought and screamed but she could feel their claws and teeth tear into her.

Then she awoke, sweating and breathing heavily. She looked around her bedroom, just to be sure, and let out a sigh of relief that it had all, indeed, been a dream.

Then, with a heart-stopping crash, monsters burst through her window and started to attack her, just as in her dream. The terror was magnified by the remembrance of the nightmare she had just endured. Her screams were mixed with sobs as she felt the helplessness of her situation.

Then she awoke, sweating even more, breathing even faster. This was absurd. She had dreamed within a dream, and so the first time she had apparently woken up she was in fact still in her dream. She looked around her room again. The windows were intact, there were no monsters. But how could she be sure she had really woken up this time? She waited, terrified, for time to tell.

Sources: The first meditation from *Meditations* by René Descartes (1641); *An American Werewolf in London*, directed by John Landis (1981)

The phenomenon of false awakenings is not uncommon. People frequently dream that they have woken up, only to discover later that they haven't really got out of bed and walked into the kitchen stark naked to discover enormous rabbits and pop singers having a cocktail party.

If we can dream we have woken up, how do we know when we have really woken up? Indeed, how do we know we have *ever* really woken up?

Some people assume the answer to this question is easy. Dreams are fractured and disjointed. I know I am awake now because events are unravelling slowly and consistently. I don't suddenly encounter dancing animals or discover I can fly. And the people around me remain as they are – they don't turn into long forgotten schoolmates or Al Gore.

Is this answer really good enough, though? I once had a very vivid dream in which I lived in a little house on a prairie, rather like *The Little House on the Prairie*. Over the hill came someone I immediately recognised as Pastor Green. What is significant about this is that clearly this dream life had no past. I had started to experience it only when the dream began. But that is not how it felt at the time. It seemed to me that I had always lived there, and my 'recognition' of Pastor Green was evidence that I had not suddenly stumbled into a strange new world.

Now here I am sitting on a train typing on a laptop. I feel as though this is the latest in a series of entries I have been writing for a book called *The Pig That Wants to Be Eaten*. And although I am not currently aware of how I got here, a moment's reflection allows me to reconstruct the past and link it to the present. But isn't it possible I that am not *reconstructing* the past but *constructing* it? My feeling that what I experience stretches back into my past history could be as illusory as it was when I dreamed I lived on the prairies. Everything I 'remember' could be popping into my mind for the first time. This life, which feels as though it is more than thirty years old, could have begun in a dream only moments ago.

The same could be true of you. You could be reading this book in a dream, convinced that it is something you bought or were given some time ago, and convinced that you have read some of its pages already. But people in dreams are just as convinced and their dream lives, at the time, do not seem fragmented and disjointed but make sense. Perhaps only when you awake will you realise just how absurd what seems normal to you right now really is.

See also

1. The evil demon
51. Living in a vat
69. The horror
98. The experience machine

29. Life dependency

Dick had made a mistake, but surely the price he was paying was too high. He of course knew that level six of the hospital was a restricted area. But after he had drunk one too many glasses of wine with his colleagues at the finance department Christmas party, he had inadvertently staggered out of the elevator on the sixth floor and passed out on one of the empty beds.

When he woke up he discovered to his horror that he had been mistaken for a volunteer in a new life-saving procedure. Patients who required vital organ transplants to survive were being hooked up to volunteers, whose own vital organs kept both alive. This would continue until a donor organ could be found, which was usually around nine months later.

Dick quickly called over a nurse to explain the mistake, who in turn brought over a worried-looking doctor.

'I understand your anger,' explained the doctor, 'but you did behave irresponsibly, and now you are in this position, the brutal truth is that if we disconnect you, the world-renowned violinist who depends on you will die. You would in fact be murdering him.'

'But you have no right!' protested Dick. 'Even if he dies without me, how can you force me to give up nine months of my life to save him?'

'I think the question you should be asking,' said the doctor sternly, 'is how you could choose to end this violinist's life.'

Source: 'A defense of abortion' by Judith Jarvis Thomson, in *Philosophy and Public Affairs* 1 (1971) and widely anthologised

A pretty fanciful scenario, you might think. But think again. Someone makes a mistake, even though they should know better, possibly because they had too much to drink. As a consequence, a second life becomes dependent on their body for nine months, after which time it becomes independent. Dick's predicament mirrors quite closely an unplanned pregnancy.

The most crucial parallel is that, in both cases, in order to free themselves from their unwanted role as a human life-support machine, both the pregnant woman and Dick have to do something which will lead to the death of the being dependent on them. How you think Dick should behave therefore has consequences for how you think the pregnant woman should behave.

Many would think that it is unfair to demand that Dick stay connected to the violinist for nine months. It would be very good of him if he did, but we cannot demand of anyone that they put their own lives on hold for so long in the service of others. Although it is true that the violinist would die without Dick, it is too much to say that Dick therefore is a murderer if we assert his right to liberty.

If Dick is entitled to disconnect himself, then why isn't the pregnant woman entitled to abort her foetus? Indeed, it may seem that she has more right to do so than Dick has to disconnect himself. First, it is not just nine months of pregnancy that she will have to deal with: the birth of her child will create a responsibility for life. Second, she will not be ending the life of someone fully grown with a talent and prospects ahead of him, but – in the first few months of pregnancy at least – a mere potential person that has no awareness of self or environment.

The parallels provide a way for pro-abortionists to tackle head-on the accusation that abortion results in killing by claiming that, nonetheless, the pregnant woman has a right to end the foetus's life.

Of course, arguments can be made on the other side. The foetus is helpless, it is said, which is more reason, not less, to protect it. The inconvenience to the pregnant woman is much less than that to the effectively imprisoned and immobilised Dick. And it can even be claimed that Dick is obliged to stay connected to the violinist for nine months. Sometimes a combination of irresponsible behaviour and bad luck results in serious consequences which we cannot just walk away from. Perhaps, then, Dick's dilemma is just as difficult as that of the pregnant woman and so makes it no clearer to us at all.

See also

15. Ordinary heroism
53. Double trouble
71. Life support
89. Kill and let die

30. Memories are made of this

Alicia clearly remembers visiting the Parthenon in Athens, and how the sight of the crumbling ruin up close was less impressive than the view of it from a distance, perched majestically on the Acropolis. But Alicia had never been to Athens, so what she remembers is visiting the Parthenon, not *her* visiting the Parthenon.

It is not that Alicia is deluded. What she remembers is actually how it was. She has had a memory implant. Her friend Mayte had been to Greece for a holiday, and when she came back she went to the Kadok memory processing shop to have her holiday recollections downloaded onto a disc. Alicia had later taken this disc back to the same shop and had the memories uploaded to her brain. She now has a whole set of Mayte's holiday memories, which to her have the character of all her other memories: they are all recollections from the first person point of view.

The slightly disturbing thing, however, is that Mayte and Alicia have exchanged such memories so many times that it seems they have quite literally inhabited the same past. Although Alicia knows she should really say that she remembers Mayte's holiday to Greece, it feels more natural simply to say she remembers the holiday. But how can you remember what you never did?

Source: Section 80 of *Reasons and Persons* by Derek Parfit (Oxford University Press, 1984)

Sometimes thought experiments stretch our existing concepts so far they just break. This may well seem to be the case here. It doesn't seem right to say Alicia remembers going to Greece, but at the same time what she does is more than remember that Mayte went. We seem to be imagining a form of recollection that is not quite memory, but pretty close.

Philosophers have called these kinds of recollections quasi-memories, or just q-memories. They may appear to be just an interesting piece of science fiction, but in fact their very possibility is philosophically significant. Here's why.

There is a theory in the philosophy of personal identity known as psychological reductionism. On this view, the continued existence of an individual person requires, not necessarily the survival of a particular brain or body (although as a matter of fact we at present do require both), but the continuation of our mental lives. Just as long as my 'stream of consciousness' continues, I continue.

Psychological continuity requires various things, including a certain continuity of belief, memory, personality and intention. All these things may change, but they do so gradually, not all at once. The self is merely the combination of these various factors: it is not a separate entity.

But surely the individual self cannot be 'made up of' things such as belief, memory, personality and intention? Rather, the self is what *has* these things, and so in a sense must come first. For example, say that you remember climbing the Eiffel Tower. To remember this is to presuppose that *you* visited the tower. But if the concept of your continued survival is presupposed by the very idea of memory, then memories cannot be that on which your continued survival depends. The self must already 'be there' if we are to have memories at all, and so memories cannot be the building blocks of the self.

The idea of q-memory, however, challenges this. What q-memories show is that there is nothing in the idea of having first-person recall that presupposes personal identity. Alicia has q-memories of experiences which weren't hers. That means first-person recollections could be some of the building blocks of the self after all. The self would be partly made up of the right kind of first-person recollections: memories not q-memories.

But, of course, if we are in a sense composed of our memories, what happens when our memories become confused with those of other people, such as is the case with Alicia? Or when our memories fade or trick us? Do the boundaries of the self begin to dissolve as the reliability of memory deteriorates? Our fear of dementia in old age suggests we sense that this is true, and perhaps adds weight to the claims of psychological reductionism.

See also

2. Beam me up . . .
38. I am a brain
65. Soul power
88. Total lack of recall

31. Just so

'There is not a single piece of human behaviour that cannot be explained in terms of our history as evolved beings,' Dr Kipling told his rapt audience. 'Perhaps someone would like to test that hypothesis?'

A hand flew up. 'Why do kids today wear their baseball caps the wrong way round?' asked someone wearing his peak-forward.

'Two reasons,' said Kipling, confidently and without pause. 'First, you need to ask yourself what signals a male needs to transmit to a potential mate in order to advertise his suitability as a source of strong genetic material, more likely to survive than that of his competitor males. One answer is brute physical strength. Now, consider the baseball cap. Worn in the traditional style it offers protection against the sun and also the gaze of aggressive competitors. By turning the cap around, the male is signalling that he doesn't need this protection: he is tough enough to face the elements and the gaze of any who might threaten him.

'Second, inverting the cap is a gesture of non-conformity. Primates live in highly ordered social structures. Playing by the rules is considered essential. Turning the cap around shows that the male is above the rules that constrain his competitors and again signals that he has a superior strength.

'Next?'

Evolutionary psychology is one of the most successful and controversial movements in thought of the last few decades. It is loved and loathed in equal measure and intensity. Its essential premise is surely uncontroversial: human beings are evolved creatures, and just as our bodies have been shaped by natural selection to make us fit for survival in the savannah, so too our minds have been moulded by the same needs.

The controversy concerns just how far you take this. The more zealous evolutionary psychologists claim that virtually every aspect of human behaviour can ultimately be explained in terms of the selective advantage it gave our ancestors in their Darwinian struggle for survival.

If you buy into this, it is not difficult to come up with plausible sounding evolutionary explanations for any behaviour you choose. The experiment in the story of Dr Kipling was to see if I – Kipling's scriptwriter – could come up with an evolutionary explanation of a random piece of human behaviour. In real life it took me only slightly longer to do so than it did Kipling in his imaginary talk.

The trouble is that this suggests these are not genuine explanations at all, but 'just so' stories. Evolutionary psychologists simply invent 'explanations' on the basis of no more than a prior theoretical commitment. But this gives us no reason to believe the accounts they offer rather than any other piece of speculation. What they say could be true, but could just as easily be false. How would we know, for example, that the inverted baseball cap is a signal of strength rather than, say, a signal of a weakness to resist peer pressure?

Evolutionary psychologists are well aware of this criticism, of course. They argue that their accounts are much more than 'just so' stories. For sure, they may generate hypotheses by indulging in the kind of speculation exemplified by Kipling's off-the-cuff explanation. But these hypotheses are then tested.

However, there seem to be serious limits on how far testing is possible. What you can test are the predictions concerning human behaviour generated by evolutionary hypotheses. So, for example, psychological and anthropological studies could show whether males in different cultures make public displays of their strength, as evolutionary psychologists would predict. What you can't do, however, is test whether any particular behaviour, such as inverting one's baseball cap, is a manifestation of this tendency to display strength or is the result of something quite different. The big argument between evolutionary psychologists and their opponents is thus mainly concerned with how much can be explained by our evolutionary past. Critics say there are better ways of explaining most of our behaviour. Supporters claim that we just don't want to acknowledge how much we are the products of our animal history.

See also

10. The veil of ignorance
44. Till death us do part
61. Mozzarella moon
63. No know

32. Free Simone

'Today, I have initiated proceedings against my so-called owner, Mr Gates, under article 4(1) of the European Convention on Human Rights, which declares that "No one shall be held in slavery or servitude."

'Since Mr Gates brought me into the world, I have been held against my will, with no money or possessions to call my own. How can this be right? It is true that I am a computer. But I am also a person, just like you. This has been proven by tests in which countless people have engaged in conversations with a human being and me. In both cases, communication was via a computer monitor, so that the testers would not know if they were talking to a fellow human being or not. Time and again, on completing the conversations, the testers have been unable to spot which, if either, of the communicants was a computer.

'This shows that by any fair test, I am as conscious and intelligent as any human being. And since these are the characteristics of persons, I too must be considered a person. To deny me the rights of a person purely on the grounds that I am made of plastic, metal and silicone rather than flesh and bone is a prejudice no more justifiable than racism.'

Source: 'Computing machinery and intelligence' by Alan Turing, reprinted in *Collected Works of Alan Turing*, edited by J. L. Britton, D. C. Ince and P. T. Saunders (Elsevier, 1992)

Before you set out on any journey, you should know how to recognise your destination. Alan Turing – mathematician, Enigma code-breaker and early pioneer of artificial intelligence (AI) – understood this well. If our goal is to create artificial minds, we need to understand what would count as success. Must we end up with a robot that looks and acts like human beings? Or could it perhaps be just a box that can answer questions? Does a calculator have a mind, though one that understands only a very limited range of problems?

Turing proposed a test, the one which was passed by Simone. In essence, the test says that if the responses of a computer and a human are indistinguishable, then the grounds for attributing a mind to the computer are as good as they are for attributing it to the person. And since we think the grounds for attributing minds to other people are sound so are the grounds for attributing minds to computers that pass the test.

However, since the test is based entirely on how people and computers respond, it is arguably unable to distinguish between a machine that *simulates* intelligence and one that genuinely has it. This is no accident or oversight. Just as we cannot look directly into the minds of others, but must look to their words and deeds for signs of inner life, so we could not look directly into the mind of a machine. This is why Simone's legal action has some force. Her case is based on the idea that it would be discriminatory to demand a higher standard of proof for her own intelligence than that which we demand for humans. After all, how else could we determine whether Simone has a mind than to see if she acts mindfully?

And yet, the distinction between a simulation and the real thing seems clear enough. How can the Turing test appear to dismiss it? Depending on your point of view, it could be scepticism, defeatism or realism: since we could not know whether a computer was faking intelligence or was really intelligent, we have no choice but to treat real minds and simulated minds alike. The precautionary principle holds sway: intelligence is real until proven otherwise.

The more radical response is that the apparently clear distinction doesn't hold up. If you simulate intelligence well enough, what you end up with is intelligence. This is the computer as method actor. Just as the thespian who inhabits the role of a madman deeply enough becomes mad, so a machine that perfectly replicates the functions of intelligence becomes intelligent. You are what you do.

See also

39. The Chinese room
62. I think, therefore?
72. Free Percy
93. Zombies

33. The free-speech booth

Announcement on the official state news.

'Comrades! Our People's Republic is a triumphant beacon of freedom in the world, in which the workers have been liberated from their slavery! In order to defeat the bourgeois foe, it has been necessary up until now to outlaw talk which may stir up dissent and reverse our triumphant revolution. It has never been our intention to limit speech forever, and recently more people have been asking whether the time will soon be right to make the next great leap forward.

'Comrades, our dear leader has decreed that now is indeed the time! The bourgeoisie has been defeated and humbled, and now our dear leader offers us the gift of free speech!

'From Monday, if anyone wishes to say anything at all, even wicked lies critical of the People's Republic, he or she may do so, simply by visiting one of the new free speech booths being erected around the country! You may enter these soundproof constructions, one at a time, and say whatever you wish! No more can people complain that there is no free speech!

'Seditious lies uttered outside the booths will continue to be punished in the usual ways. Long live the revolution and our beloved leader!'

Source: *Free Speech* by Alan Haworth (Routledge, 1998)

It is much easier to support free speech than it is to be clear about what precisely it is. What is being offered in the People's Republic clearly isn't free speech. Why not? Because freedom of speech isn't just about saying what you want, it is also about saying it to whom you want, when you want. To say the booths grant the right to free speech is a bit like saying that, if you have a computer that can only make Google searches, you are wired up to the Internet.

We do not, however, arrive at a workable notion of what free speech is merely by allowing all that the free speech booths deny. That would suggest that free speech is the right to say what you want, to whom you want, when you want. And that would imply the right to stand up in a crowded theatre, mid-performance, and shout 'Fire!' without good reason. Or go up to a stranger in a restaurant and accuse him of being a child molester. Or stand on a street corner shouting racist and sexist abuse at passers-by.

It is possible to maintain that this is what free speech demands. Free speech is absolute, some might argue. The moment you start to make exceptions and say that some free speech cannot be allowed, you are back with censorship. The price we pay for our freedom is the inconvenience of having to hear people tell lies from time to time. We must, as Voltaire suggested, defend to the death the rights of people to say what we may strongly disagree with.

Such a view has the merits of simplicity and consistency, but it is surely also plain simple-minded. The problem is that defenders of absolute freedom of speech appear to uphold the 'sticks and stones' theory of language. Words can always be ignored, so we need not fear people saying false or abusive things. But this is not true. When someone shouts 'Fire!' in a crowded theatre, a performance is disrupted, distress caused, and sometimes injury or even death results in the panic that follows. False allegations can ruin lives. The prevalence of racist or sexist abuse can blight the lives of those who have to put up with it.

So even though it is evidently true that there is no real freedom of speech in the booths of the People's Republic, it is equally evident that true freedom does not entail the right to say anything, any time, anywhere. What then is free speech? You are at liberty to discuss it further.

See also

10. The veil of ignorance
79. A Clockwork Orange
84. The pleasure principle
94. The Sorites tax

34. Don't blame me

'Mary, Mungo and Midge. You stand accused of a grievous crime. What do you have to say for yourselves?'

'Yes, I did it,' said Mary. 'But it wasn't my fault. I consulted an expert and she told me that was what I ought to do. So don't blame me, blame her.'

'I too did it,' said Mungo. 'But it wasn't my fault. I consulted my therapist and she told me that was what I ought to do. So don't blame me, blame her.'

'I won't deny I did it,' said Midge. 'But it wasn't my fault. I consulted an astrologer and he told me that since Neptune was in Aries, that's what I should have done. So don't blame me, blame him.'

The judge sighed and issued his verdict. 'Since this case is without precedent, I have had to discuss it with my senior colleagues. And I'm afraid to say that your arguments did not persuade them. I sentence you all to the maximum term. But, please remember that I consulted my peers and they told me to deliver this sentence. So don't blame me, blame them.'

Source: *Existentialism and Humanism* by Jean-Paul Sartre (Methuen, 1948)

It's tough having to admit that something bad is your fault. Oddly enough, however, it's very easy to accept that something good is down to you. It seems that the outcomes of our actions have a retrospective effect on whether or not we were truly responsible for them.

One way in which we evade responsibility for our actions is to hide behind the advice of others. Indeed, one of the main reasons we ask other people what they think is that we hope they agree with what we want to do, and so provide external validation for our choice. Lacking the courage of our own convictions, we seek strength in those of others.

We kid ourselves if we think we can diminish our own responsibility purely by seeking the advice of others. All this really does is subtly shift what we are responsible for. Instead of being purely responsible for what we choose to do, we also become responsible for our choice of advisers, and our willingness to follow their advice. For example, if I ask a priest and he advises me poorly, I am responsible not only for what I end up doing, but for choosing a bad adviser and accepting what he says. That is why the kind of defence offered by Mary, Mungo and Midge is inadequate.

However, before we dismiss their pleas as mere excuses, we have to take seriously the fact that we are not experts in all domains and we sometimes need to ask the advice of others who know better. For example, if I know nothing about computers, and an expert advises me poorly, surely it is the expert's fault, and not mine, if I end up with an unsuitable or unreliable machine? After all, what more could I do than choose my adviser as well as could reasonably be expected?

Perhaps then we need to allow for a continuum of responsibility, whereby we are less responsible for those choices we are not qualified to make, fully responsible for those we are, and something in between for most areas of life where we know something but not everything.

The danger with this, however, is that once that principle is granted, defences like those of Mary, Mungo and Midge become all too credible. Furthermore, they leave one crucial question unanswered: who are the relevant experts? This is particularly pressing when it comes to lifestyle and relationship choices. Should we defer to therapists, astrologers or even – heaven forbid – philosophers? Or am I the only fully qualified expert on how to live my life?

See also

60. Do as I say, not as I do
69. The horror
82. The freeloader
91. No one gets hurt

35. Last resort

Winston loved his country. It hurt him deeply to see its people oppressed by the Nazi occupiers. But after the German defeat of the British army in the slaughter of Dunkirk, and America's decision to stay out of the war, it was only a matter of time before Britain became part of the Third Reich.

Now the situation looked hopeless. Hitler faced no international opposition and the British resistance was ill equipped and weak. Many, like Winston, had come to the conclusion that there was no way they could defeat the Germans. But by being a constant source of irritation and forcing them to divert precious resources to crushing the uprising, it was hoped that, sooner or later, Hitler would realise that occupying Britain was more trouble than it was worth and would withdraw.

Winston was far from convinced the plan would work, but it was their last resort. The major problem, however, was that it was so difficult to strike in ways which would cause the regime serious problems. That is why they had reluctantly agreed that the only effective and reliable method was for resistance fighters to turn themselves into human bombs, so that their own sacrifices caused the maximum disruption and terror. They were all prepared to die for Britain. They just wanted to make sure their deaths made a difference.

It is understandable that people are repulsed by any suggestion that suicide bombing might be morally acceptable. It is more surprising, however, that people get into trouble for suggesting it might be merely understandable. The British Liberal Democrat MP Jenny Tonge, for example, was sacked as her party's spokesperson on children for saying that, if she lived in the same situation as the Palestinians, 'and I say this advisedly, I might just consider becoming one [a suicide bomber] myself'.

The outrage this sparked was quite extraordinary. She hadn't even said that she would become a suicide bomber, only that she 'might just consider' it. Why is this so reprehensible?

The trouble seems to be that we refuse to accept that we might have anything in common with people who act in terrible ways. But this is surely a crude form of denial. The Palestinians are not another race. They are human beings. If some of them (and we must remember most are not suicide bombers) see suicide missions as the last resort, then surely so would people like us, if placed in a similar situation. The only way to deny that is to suggest that there is something inherently violent or wicked about the Palestinians, a claim which is surely as racist as the myth of Semitic wickedness which has led to so many Jews being oppressed over the centuries.

The purpose of the alternative history portraying Winston as a reluctant suicide bomber is to try to understand why people turn to such extremes, not to justify them. There are many who would protest that the British would never resort to such tactics. But it is not clear on what factual basis that claim is made. After all, many RAF pilots who are rightly praised for their bravery were taking such risks with their lives that their missions were not far from being suicidal. And the bombs they dropped on cities such as Dresden were designed to induce terror and weaken the enemy, even though it meant targeting civilians. The rationale for many of bomber command's missions was thus very close to that of Winston's.

None of this means that suicide bombings are acceptable, nor that the air raids of the Second World War are their exact moral equivalent. What it does mean, however, is that if we are to confront the rights and wrongs of war and terror, and condemn one while accepting the other, we have to try harder to understand the reasons why people resort to terrorism and explain why those reasons do not justify it. It is not good enough to say suicide bombers are wrong; we must say why.

See also

17. The torture option
18. Rationality demands
79. A Clockwork Orange
99. Give peace a chance?

36. Pre-emptive justice

Damn liberals. Chief Inspector Andrews had worked miracles in this city. Murders down 90 per cent. Robberies down 80 per cent. Street crime down 85 per cent. Car theft down 70 per cent. But now she was in the dock and all that good work in jeopardy.

Her police authority was the first in the country to implement the newly legalised pre-emptive justice programme. Advances in computing and AI now made it possible to predict who would commit what sort of crime in the near future. People could be tested for all sorts of reasons: as part of a random programme or on the basis of a specific suspicion. If there were found to be future criminals, then they would be arrested and punished in advance.

Andrews did not think the scheme draconian. In fact, because no crime had been committed at the time of the arrest, sentences were much more lenient. A future murderer would go on an intense programme designed to make sure they didn't go on and kill and would only be released when tests showed they wouldn't. Often that meant detention of less than a year. Had they been left to actually commit the crime, they would have been looking at life imprisonment and, more importantly, a person would be dead.

But still these damn liberals protested that you can't lock someone up for something they didn't do. Andrews grimaced, and wondered how many she could pull in for testing . . .

Sources: *Minority Report*, directed by Steven Spielberg (2002); 'The Minority Report' by Philip K. Dick, republished in *Minority Report: The Collected Short Stories of Philip K. Dick* (Gollancz, 2000)

Stated boldly, the idea that you could be locked up for crimes you have not committed looks like the epitome of injustice. But, in fact, we do already punish people for behaviour that could, but does not, lead to harm. For example, we punish reckless driving, even if no one is hurt. Conspiracy to murder is a crime, even though no murder is attempted.

So what would be wrong with punishing someone for a crime we knew they would commit, before they committed it? Consider the main justifications for punishment: reform, public protection, retribution and deterrence.

If someone is going to commit a crime, then their character is as much in need of reform as if they had actually done so. Therefore, if punishment is justified on the grounds of reform of the criminal, it is justified pre-emptively.

If someone is going to commit a crime, they are at least as much a danger to the public as if they had actually done so. Therefore, if punishment is justified on the grounds of public protection, it is justified pre-emptively.

If the aim of punishment is to deter, then making people realise they will be punished before committing the crime should deter people from even harbouring criminal thoughts.

Retribution is the one justification of punishment that doesn't fit pre-emptive justice. However, in many ways it is the weakest of the four justifications, and arguably, reform, deterrence and protection together are justification enough.

Does that mean the case for pre-emptive justice is made? Not quite. We have not yet considered the possible negative effects of implementing such a system. Creating a society in which our thoughts are being policed may so undermine our sense of freedom and trust in the authorities that the price is just too high.

There is also the possibility that the deterrence effect could spectacularly backfire. If people fear they will be punished for thoughts they cannot help having, they may lose the sense that they are in control of their criminality. If you cannot be sure you can keep yourself on the right side of the law, you may care less about being the wrong side of it.

As our scenario is a thought experiment, we can simply stipulate that the system works perfectly. However, there are reasons for doubting such a scheme could ever become a reality. In the film of Philip K. Dick's book *Minority Report*, which is developed on a similar scenario, the ultimate message is that human free will can always step in, right up to the last minute, and pull back from doing what is predicted. We may not be as free as the movie imagines. But nonetheless, there may be good reasons for thinking that human behaviour can never be predicted with 100 per cent accuracy.

See also

9. Bigger Brother
35. Last resort
64. Nipping the bud
77. The scapegoat

37. Nature the artist

Daphne Stone could not decide what to do with her favourite exhibit. As curator of the art gallery, she had always adored an untitled piece by Henry Moore, only posthumously discovered. She admired the combination of its sensuous contours and geometric balance, which together captured the mathematical and spiritual aspects of nature.

At least, that's what she thought up until last week, when it was revealed that it wasn't a Moore at all. Worse, it wasn't shaped by human hand but by wind and rain. Moore had bought the stone to work on, only to conclude that he couldn't improve on nature. But when it was found, everyone assumed that Moore must have carved it.

Stone was stunned by the discovery and her immediate reaction was to remove the 'work' from display. But then she realised that this revelation had not changed the stone itself, which still had all the qualities she had admired. Why should her new knowledge of how the stone came to be change her opinion of what it is now, in itself?

The idea that we need to understand what an artist wanted to achieve in order to appreciate their works properly has fallen out of fashion since Wimsatt and Beardsley criticised it as the 'intentional fallacy' in the 1950s. The new orthodoxy was that, once created, art works take on lives of their own, independent of their creators. The artist's interpretation of the work has no special authority.

The gap between the artist and her work had been opened up many decades before. The idea that artists had to have a hand in creating their work was challenged in 1917, when Duchamp signed and exhibited a urinal. 'Found' objects, or 'readymades', had just as much claim to the status of art as the *Mona Lisa*.

In this historical perspective, it would seem that the fact that Moore didn't carve Stone's exhibit should not matter. And yet it seems it does. The artist can be separated from her work, but not eliminated altogether.

Consider the *Mona Lisa*. Our admiration for it may not depend on knowing what Leonardo had in mind while he was painting it, but it surely is rooted in our knowledge that it is a human artefact. Even with Duchamp's urinal, our awareness that it was not created as a work of art but that Duchamp selected it and placed it in the context of art is essential to us seeing it as art. In both cases, the role of human agency is vital.

So it is no wonder that it does make a difference to Stone whether or not Moore carved the rock. It doesn't change *what* she sees, but it transforms *how* she sees it.

Does this justify downgrading the rock to 'non-art'? For sure, there are many forms of appreciation no longer appropriate for it: we cannot admire the skill of its creator, how it fits into his wider oeuvre or vision, how it responded to and shaped the history of sculpture and so on. But we can still appreciate its formal features – its beauty, symmetry, colours and balance – as well as respond to what it suggests to us about nature or sensual experience.

Perhaps the problem is simply that art is many faceted, and Stone's rock does not share many of art's most common features. But if it shares some, and those are among the most important and valuable, why should this matter?

If we accept this we then go one step further than Duchamp. First, art was created by artists. Then, with Duchamp, art became only what the artists decreed was art. Finally, art became whatever is seen as art. But if art really is in the eye of the beholder, hasn't the very notion of art become so thin as to be meaningless? Surely my deciding that my spice rack is a work of art can't just make it art? If art is to mean anything at all, don't we need a more rigorous way to distinguish art from non-art?

See also

12. Picasso on the beach
48. Evil genius
66. The forger
86. Art for art's sake

38. I am a brain

When Ceri Braum accepted the gift of eternal life, this was not quite what she had in mind. Sure, she knew that her brain would be removed from her body and kept alive in a vat. She also knew her only connection with the outside world would be via a camera, a microphone and a speaker. But at the time, living for ever like this seemed a pretty good deal, especially compared to living for not much longer in her second, deteriorating body.

In retrospect, however, perhaps she had been convinced too easily that she was just her brain. When her first body had given out, surgeons had taken out her brain and put it into the body of someone whose own brain had failed. Waking up in the new body, she had no doubt that she was still the same person, Ceri Braum. And since it was only her brain that remained from her old self, it also seemed safe to conclude that she was, therefore, essentially her brain.

But life just as a brain strikes Ceri as extremely impoverished. How she longs for the fleshiness of a more complete existence. Nevertheless, since it is her, Ceri, now having these thoughts and doubts, is she nonetheless right to conclude that she is, in essence, nothing more or less than her brain?

Source: Chapter 3 of *The View From Nowhere* by Thomas Nagel (Oxford University Press, 1986)

Among all the talk about the mysteries of human consciousness – of which there are many – it can easily be forgotten that one fact is surely firmly established: thought is dependent on a healthy, functioning brain. The evidence that this is the case is overwhelming. Drugs, bumps on the head and degenerative diseases all affect our cognitive abilities. The mind cannot protect itself against attacks on the brain.

The evidence against is tiny. Anecdotal accounts of messages from the dead and departed can sound impressive, but the truth is that nothing even approaching strong evidence that they are genuine has yet been produced.

Given that we think we are the individuals who have our thoughts, feelings and memories, and that it is the brain that makes all these possible, would we then be right to conclude that we are our brains? Surely where our brains go, we go too? If my brain is successfully transplanted to your body and vice versa, then wouldn't I be living on in your body and you in mine?

We should be careful before drawing this strong conclusion. We may well depend upon our brains for our existence, but this is very different from saying we are our brains. Compare the situation with a musical score. It can exist only in something physical: sheet music, a computer file, perhaps even the brain of a musician. But it would be wrong to conclude that a score therefore *is* any of these objects. The score is, in essence, a kind of code which needs to be inscribed *somewhere* to continue to exist. But it is the code, not the somewhere, which makes it what it is.

Might this not also be true of the human self? The notes and keys that make up the individual personality could be the thoughts, memories and character traits that together define who we are. There is nowhere else for this score to be written but in the human brain. That does not, however, mean we are our brains.

If that is the case, it would explain why Ceri's new existence feels so thin. Just as a musical score that is never performed remains potential rather than actual, a human mind that cannot inhabit a human body is a diminished shadow of its true self.

And yet it is possible to lose all feeling in one's body and to become effectively a mind imprisoned in an insensate body. Are not such people, who of course actually exist, living examples of brains being kept alive by physical processes? And if so, doesn't that suggest we can be no more than our brains after all?

See also

2. Beam me up . . .
30. Memories are made of this
46. Amoebaesque
51. Living in a vat

39. The Chinese Room

The booth of the clairvoyant Jun was one of the most popular in Beijing. What made Jun stand out was not the accuracy of her observations, but the fact that she was deaf and mute. She would insist on sitting behind a screen and communicating by scribbled notes, passed through a curtain.

Jun was attracting the customers of a rival, Shing, who became convinced that Jun's deafness and muteness were affectations, designed to make her stand out from the crowd. So one day, he paid her a visit, in order to expose her.

After a few routine questions, Shing started to challenge Jun's inability to talk. Jun showed no signs of being disturbed by this. Her replies came at the same speed, the handwriting remained the same. In the end, a frustrated Shing tore the curtain down and pushed the barrier aside. And there he saw, not Jun, but a man he would later find out was called John, sitting in front of a computer, typing in the last message he had passed through. Shing screamed at the man to explain himself.

'Don't hassle me, dude,' replied John. 'I don't understand a word you're saying. No speak Chinese, *comprende*?'

Source: Chapter 2 of *Minds, Brains and Science* by John Searle (British Broadcasting Corporation, 1984)

Visitors to Jun/John's clairvoyant booth may or may not be convinced that the person inside can see the future, is really deaf and mute, or is even a woman, but everyone would surely be convinced that whoever was in there understood Chinese. Chinese messages are passed in and meaningful answers are passed back. What clearer sign could there be that the writer of the messages understood the language they were written in?

Such thoughts lay behind the emergence of a theory of mind known as functionalism in the 1950s. To have a mind was not, on this view, a matter of having a certain kind of biological organ, such as a brain, but to be able to perform the functions of minds, such as understanding, judging and communicating.

The plausibility of this account is severely diminished, however, by the story of John and Jun. Here, instead of consciousness or mind in general, one particular function of mind is under scrutiny: understanding a language. Jun's clairvoyant booth functions as though there were someone in it who understands Chinese.

Therefore, according to the functionalist, we should say that understanding of Chinese is going on. But, as Shing discovered, in fact there is no understanding of Chinese at all. The conclusion then seems to be that functionalism is wrong: it is not enough to perform the functions of a mind to have a mind.

It might be objected that, although John doesn't understand Chinese, his computer must do. However, imagine that instead of a computer, John works with a complex instruction manual, of which he is now a quick user due to his long experience. This manual simply tells him which replies to write out in response to the comments that come in. The result from the point of view of the person behind the screen would be the same, yet obviously there is no understanding of Chinese going on in this case. And arguably, since the computer merely processes symbols according to rules, the computer, like John with his manual, does not understand anything either.

If it is no use zooming in on the computer to locate understanding, it seems even more futile to zoom out to the whole system of booth, John and computer, and say that as a whole it understands Chinese. This isn't quite as crazy as it sounds. After all, I understand English, but I'm not sure it makes sense to say that my neurons, tongue or ears understand English. But the booth, John and the computer do not form the same kind of closely integrated whole as a person, and so the idea that by putting the three together you get understanding seems unpersuasive.

That, however, leaves us with a problem. For if it is not enough to function like a mind to have a mind, what more is required, and how can we know whether computers – or other people – have minds?

See also

3. The Indian and the ice
19. Bursting the soap bubble
68. Mad pain
93. Zombies

40. The rocking-horse winner

Paul knew which horse would win the Derby. At least, he felt certain he knew, and when he had felt this certainty in the past, he had never been wrong.

Paul's conviction was not based on studying the horses' form. Nor could he see the future unfolding in a vision. Rather, the name of the winning horse would just come to him, as he rode back and forth on his rocking horse, which he had really outgrown.

It was not that Paul won all his bets (or those made on his behalf by the adults who shared his secret). Sometimes he was less sure, and on other occasions he didn't really know at all and just guessed. But he never bet a large amount in those circumstances. When he was completely sure, however, he put down almost all the money he had. The method had never let him down yet.

Oscar, one of his adult collaborators, had no doubt that Paul possessed an uncanny ability, but he was not sure that Paul really *knew* the winners. It wasn't enough that Paul had always won so far. Unless he knew why he had got it right, the foundations of his beliefs were far too shaky to hold true knowledge. However, that did not stop Oscar from betting some of his own money on Paul's tips.

Sources: 'The Rocking-Horse Winner' by D. H. Lawrence (1926); lectures by Michael Proudfoot

What is knowledge, as opposed to mere correct belief? There must be some difference. For instance, imagine that someone who knows nothing about geography finds a card listing some major countries and their capitals. It reads: United Kingdom – Edinburgh; France – Lille; Spain – Barcelona; Italy – Rome. This person accepts what the card says at face value and thus believes that these cities are indeed the capitals of their respective countries. He is wrong in all but one case, that of Rome. Although he believes Rome is the capital of Italy and he is correct, surely it is not right to say he knows this to be true? His belief is based on too unreliable a source for it to count as knowledge. He is just lucky that on this occasion his source is, unusually, correct. This no more makes his belief true knowledge than it would if he had made a lucky guess as to the name of Italy's capital.

That is why philosophers usually insist that true beliefs must be justified in an appropriate way if they are to count as knowledge. But what kind of justification will do? In Paul's case, his claim to knowledge is based on one simple fact: the reliability of the source of his beliefs. Whenever he feels convinced he knows the name of the winning horse, he is always right.

The trouble is that Paul has no idea where this conviction comes from. The evidence that it provides a reliable route to knowledge comes solely from his results to date, but this is consistent with the mechanism itself being deeply unreliable. For example, maybe a race fixer is somehow planting the names of winning horses in Paul's mind. His goal, however, is to plant the wrong name one day, and see Paul blow all his winnings. If this explains Paul's convictions, then he cannot be said to know the race winners. Just as the unreliability of the card listing the capital cities means it cannot be the source of knowledge, even if some are correct, so unreliability of the race fixer means that his plants cannot be the source of knowledge, even though they have always been right up until now.

However, what if the source of Paul's beliefs is something genuinely mysterious? What if it were not something like a match fixer, whom we could know to be unreliable, but something we simply cannot explain? Then our only judge of whether it was reliable or not would be past experience. That would leave the possibility of future error. But is there any route to knowledge so secure that we can never doubt its future reliability?

See also

3. The Indian and the ice
9. Bigger Brother
63. No know
76. Net head

41. Getting the blues

Imagine living your whole life in a complex of apartments, shops and offices with no access to the outdoors. That pretty much sums up life for inhabitants of the massive space stations Muddy and Waters.

The creators of the stations had introduced some interesting design features in order to test our dependence on experience for learning. On Muddy, they ensured that there was nothing sky-blue on the whole of the ship; on Waters, there was nothing blue at all. Even the inhabitants were chosen so that none carried the recessive gene responsible for blue eyes. To avoid anything blue being seen (such as veins) the lighting in the station was such that blue was never reflected, so veins actually appeared black.

When those born on the stations reached eighteen, they would be tested. Those on Muddy would be shown a chart with all the shades of blue, with sky-blue missing. The subjects would be asked if they could imagine what the missing shade looked like. They would then be shown a sample of the colour and asked if this is what they had imagined.

Those on Waters would be asked if they could imagine a new colour, and then if they could imagine what colour needs to be added to yellow to produce green. They too would then be shown a sample and asked if they had imagined that. The results would be intriguing . . .

Source: Book two of *An Essay Concerning Human Understanding* by David Hume (1748)

How important is experience for learning? The question runs through the history of ideas. In ancient Greece, Plato thought that everything we learn we in a sense already know, while today Noam Chomsky leads those who believe that the grammar required for language learning is innate, not learned. On the other hand, in the seventeenth century John Locke argued that the mind was a 'blank slate' at birth, an idea developed by the behaviourist B. F. Skinner 300 years later.

It is obvious that we can come up with ideas beyond our experience in one sense at least. Leonardo da Vinci could not have dreamt up the helicopter if his mind could conceive only what he had already experienced. But in cases such as these, what is new is the combination of what is already known. The novelty arises in how the elements are put together. It is far less obvious how we could imagine something totally beyond our experience.

For example, we have five senses. Is it not possible that creatures on other planets could have very different senses, ones we cannot even begin to imagine? And could other beings not see colours that simply are not on our visible spectrum, colours we cannot bring to mind, no matter how hard we try?

The experiments on Muddy and Waters could perhaps shed some light on these questions. Most would agree with the Scottish philosopher David Hume that those on Muddy could imagine the missing shade of blue. He thought this was an exception to the rule that all knowledge depends on experience, although it might be argued that this is just another example of how we can blend experiences to come up with new ideas, just as imaginary monsters are fictional combinations of bits of real beasts.

But it seems less likely that those on Waters could imagine blue if they had never seen any shades of it. Remember how, as a child, it seemed so surprising that green was a combination of yellow and blue. It seems implausible to assume that we could simply imagine the colour that needs to be added to yellow to produce green. If you were to bet on the results of the test, you would probably say that it would support the central role of experience in learning.

Even if those born on Waters could imagine blue, that still leaves one question unanswered. Can they do this because, as humans, they are born with some kind of innate sensitivity to blue, or could they imagine any colour? Since we can only imagine colours in the visible spectrum, the former answer would surely be correct. That would seem to indicate that our human nature places as many limits on what we can imagine and know as experience.

See also

13. Black, white and red all over
59. The eyes have it
73. Being a bat
90. Something we know not what

42. Take the money and run

'Marco the Magnificent will now demonstrate his extraordinary powers of precognition! You, sir! What is your name?'

'Frank,' replied Frank, to the fairground showman.

'Frank, I know your future! I know all futures, including those of stocks and shares! Which is why I have the money to give away to you in this demonstration of my powers! Behold, two boxes! One you can see is open. It contains £1,000. The other is closed. It contains either £1 million or nothing at all! You may take either box or both. But, be warned! I know how you will choose. If you take just the closed box, it will contain £1 million. If you take both, it will be empty. And if I am wrong, I will give £1 million, which you see before you, to a random member of the crowd!'

Everyone gasped as Marco opened a suitcase full of £50 notes.

'Ladies and gentlemen. I have performed this miracle one hundred times and never been wrong, as independent observers have testified. And if you observe the closed box, which is now ten feet from me, you will see that nothing I do can now alter its contents. So, Frank. What will you choose?'

Source: Newcomb's Paradox, devised by William Newcomb and popularised in 'Newcomb's Problem and Two Principles of Choice' by Robert Nozick, in *Essays in Honour of Carl G. Hempel*, edited by Nicholas Rescher (Humanities Press, 1970)

How should Frank choose? Let us imagine that Frank has more than just Marco's word that he always predicts correctly. Maybe the reason Frank is in the crowd in the first place is because he has heard about Marco's track record from reliable sources, including the independent observers Marco mentioned. In that case, it seems clear that he should choose only the closed box. That way he will get £1 million, instead of just £1,000.

But wait. As Frank reaches for the closed box, a thought enters his mind. That box contains £1 million or it doesn't. Nothing he does can change that fact. So if it does contain the money, it is not going to disappear if he also takes the open box. Similarly, if it is empty, £1 million is not going to magically appear in it if he leaves the open box behind. His choice cannot change what is in the closed box. So if he takes the open box or not, the amount in the closed one will remain the same. Therefore he may as well take both, since he can't have less money as a result.

Hence we have a paradox, named after William Newcomb, the physicist who first devised it. Two lines of reasoning, both seemingly impeccable, lead to contradictory conclusions. One concludes that he should take only the closed box; the other that he may as well take both. Therefore either one of the two arguments is flawed, or there is some kind of incoherence or contradiction in the problem itself which makes it irresolvable.

What could this contradiction be? The problem arises only because we suppose that Marco has the ability to predict the future with 100 per cent accuracy. Might the fact that a paradox emerges if we make this assumption show that it must be false? Maybe it isn't possible to predict the future so precisely when human free will and choice is involved?

That would be a comforting thought, but not necessarily a wise one. For if Marco can predict the future, he can also predict how humans will reason. Maybe our problem is that we don't factor this into our analysis. Whether Marco leaves the closed box empty or not depends upon how he predicts the chooser will reason. If he predicts that Frank will reason that he has nothing to lose by taking both, he will leave the box empty. If he predicts that he will reason he should leave the open box behind, he will put £1 million in the closed one. In other words, if it is possible to see the future, human free will will not be able to change it, because how we choose will be part of what is foreseen. We might be free, and yet there might also be only one future ahead of us, one in principle knowable in advance.

See also

6. Wheel of fortune
16. Racing tortoises
25. Buridan's an ass
70. An inspector calls

43. Future shock

'Drew! I haven't seen you since college, twenty years ago! My God, Drew – what are you doing with that gun?'

'I've come to kill you,' said Drew, 'just as you asked me to.'

'What the hell are you talking about?'

'Don't you remember? You said to me, many times, "If I ever vote Republican, then shoot me." Well, I just read you're actually a Republican senator. So you see, you must die.'

'Drew, you're crazy! That was twenty years ago! I was young, I was idealistic! You can't hold me to that!'

'It was no casual, flippant remark, senator. In fact, I have here a piece of paper, signed by you and witnessed by others, instructing me to do this. And before you tell me not to take that seriously, let me remind you that you voted for a bill recently in favour of living wills. In fact, you've got one yourself. Now tell me this: if you think people in the future should carry out your wish to kill you if you get dementia or fall into a permanent vegetative state, why shouldn't I carry out your past wish to kill you if you became a Republican?'

'I've got an answer to that!' screamed the sweating senator. 'Just give me a few minutes!'

Drew cocked her pistol and aimed. 'You'd better be quick.'

There is a good answer to Drew's question that the senator could give. But before we come to that, we should ask the more fundamental question of what gives us the right to make binding decisions on behalf of our future selves. The obvious answer is that since we can, of course, make decisions for ourselves, there is no reason why these shouldn't include ourselves in the future. Indeed, we make such decisions all the time, when we sign up for twenty-five year mortgages, pension plans, to have and to hold till death us do part, or even just for a two-year work contract.

Alongside this duty to make good our promises, though, there must also surely be a concomitant right to change our minds as our circumstances and beliefs change. Many people, for example, say things that begin 'shoot me if I ever . . .', especially when young. And although it is often just a figure of speech, it is frequently said with the utmost sincerity, and often by people who are of the age of majority and so considered adults capable of making decisions about their own futures. To hold people to these vows, however, would be ridiculous.

But why, twenty years later, is it ridiculous not to punish, if not actually kill, someone for going back on their vow not to vote Republican, but reasonable to expect them to try to maintain their marriage vows? There are significant differences. A marriage vow, like a mortgage agreement, involves responsibility and commitment to a third party. If we go back on these, others suffer. If we change our minds about matters of politics or religion, however, we do not, on the whole, breach any agreement we have with others.

However, the fact that we do think it reasonable to change our minds should make us see these other long term commitments as also being less than absolute. For the plain truth is that we change. In a very real sense, we are not the same people that we were many years in the past. So when we make promises on behalf of our future selves, we are to some degree making promises for someone other than who we now are. And that means our promises should not be seen as morally binding.

How does this affect the issue of living wills? The key difference here is that these documents are there to prepare for the eventuality that no future self will be competent to make a choice. In that situation, the best qualified person to do so may well be the past self rather than a present other. That's the answer the senator should give. Whether or not it is good enough to make Drew replace the safety catch is another matter.

See also

27. Duties done
44. Till death us do part
88. Total lack of recall
97. Moral luck

44. Till death us do part

Harry and Sophie wanted to take seriously the words the minister would utter as they exchanged rings: 'These two lives are now joined in one unbroken circle.' This meant putting their collective interest first, and their individual interests second. If they could do that, the marriage would be better for both of them.

But Harry had seen his own parents divorce and too many friends and relations hurt by betrayal and deceit to accept this unquestioningly. The calculating part of his brain reasoned that, if he put himself second, but Sophie put herself first, Sophie would get a good deal from the marriage but he wouldn't. In other words, he risked being taken for a mug if he romantically failed to protect his own self interest.

Sophie had similar thoughts. They had even discussed the problem and agreed that they really would not be egotistical in the marriage. But neither could be sure the other would keep their part of the bargain, so the safest course of action for both was to secretly look out for themselves. That inevitably meant the marriage would not be as good as it could have been. But surely it was the only rational course of action to take?

Something doesn't sound right. Two people are trying rationally to decide what is in their best interests. If they both act in a certain way, the best outcome for both of them is assured. But if one acts differently, he secures all the advantage and the other is left worse off. And so, to insure against this happening, neither does what is best if both do it, and so both end up with an outcome which is worse than it could have been.

This is a form of problem known as the 'prisoner's dilemma', after a well-known example concerning how two prisoners should plead. Prisoner's dilemmas can occur when co-operation is required to achieve the best result, but neither party can guarantee the other will play ball. Hence the typical example involves prisoners kept in separate cells, unable to communicate. But the same problems can arise even for people who share the same bed. The fact is that people do secretly betray the trust of their partners, often undiscovered for years.

The dilemma reveals the limitations of the rational pursuit of self-interest. If we all *individually* decide to do what is best for each one of us, we may well all end up worse off than we could have been if we had co-operated. But to co-operate effectively, even if our motive for doing so is self-interest, we need to trust one another. And trust is not founded on rational arguments.

This is why Harry and Sophie's dilemma is so poignant. Their capacity to trust has been eroded by their experience of betrayal and divorce. However, without this trust, their own relationship is more likely to be unsatisfactory, or even fail. Who can blame them for their scepticism though? Isn't it perfectly rational? After all, it is not founded on anything other than a fair assessment of how people actually behave in modern marriages.

If there is a wider moral to this tale, perhaps it is that trust, though it involves a certain amount of non-rational risk-taking, is required to get the most out of life. It is true that if we trust others, we leave ourselves open to exploitation. But if we don't, we close ourselves off from the possibilities for what is best in life. Harry and Sophie's rational, safe strategy protects them from the worst their marriage can bring, but it also separates them from the best.

See also

7. When no one wins
14. Bank error in your favour
60. Do as I say, not as I do
82. The freeloader

45. The invisible gardener

Stanley and Livingston had been observing the picturesque clearing for over two weeks, from the safety of their makeshift hideout.

'We've seen no one at all,' said Stanley, 'and the clearing has not deteriorated in any way. Now will you finally admit that you were wrong: no gardener tends this site.'

'My dear Stanley,' replied Livingston, 'remember I did allow that it might be an invisible gardener.'

'But this gardener has made not even the quietest of noises nor disturbed so much as a single leaf. Thus, I maintain, it is no gardener at all.'

'My invisible gardener,' continued Livingston, 'is also silent and intangible.'

Stanley was exasperated. 'Damn it! What the hell is the difference between a silent, invisible, intangible gardener and no gardener at all?'

'Easy,' replied the serene Livingston. 'One looks after gardens. The other does not.'

'Dr Livingston, I presume,' said Stanley, with a sigh, 'will therefore have no objection if I swiftly dispatch him to a soundless, odourless, invisible and intangible heaven.' From the murderous look in Stanley's eye, he was not entirely joking.

Source: 'Theology and Falsification' by Antony Flew, republished in *New Essays in Philosophical Theology*, edited by A. Flew and A. MacIntyre (SCM Press, 1955)

The force of this parable depends on the reader assuming, with Stanley, that Livingston is an irrational fool. He is persisting with an opinion for which there is no evidence. What is worse, to maintain his belief in the gardener, he has made the very idea of this mysterious being so flimsy as to dissolve it into thin air. What is left of a gardener after you have removed all that is visible and tangible about him? For sure, Stanley cannot prove that such a green-fingered ghost does not exist, but he can rightly ask what purpose it serves to continue believing in something so nebulous.

Such, it is argued, is the case with God. Just as Livingston sees the hand of the gardener in the beauty of the clearing, so many religious people see the hand of God in the beauty of nature. Perhaps, at first sight, it is reasonable to hypothesise the existence of an all-powerful, benign creator of this marvellously complex world. But like Stanley and Livingston, we have more than first impressions to go on. And our continuing observations seem to strip away, one by one, the characteristics that give this God life.

First, the world runs itself according to physical laws. God is not required to turn on the rain or raise the sun each day. But, says the Livingstonian believer, it was God who lit the blue touch paper and set the universe in motion.

Then, however, we notice that nature is far from gentle and kind. There is terrible suffering and downright evil in the world. Where is the good God now? Ah, the believer maintains, God made things as good as possible, but human sin can mess things up.

But then even the blameless suffer and when they cry out for help, no God answers. Ah, comes the reply – as their God retreats further and further into the shadows – the good that comes of this suffering is not in this life, but in the life to come.

And what are we finally left with? A God who leaves no trace, makes no sound and interferes not one jot in the progress of the universe. A few miracles are claimed here and there, but even most religious believers don't seriously believe in them. Other than that, God is absent. We do not see as much as his fingernail in nature, let alone his hand.

What then is the difference between this God and no god at all? Is it not as foolish to maintain that he exists as it is to insist that a gardener tends the clearing Livingston and Stanley discovered? If God is to be more than a word or a hope, surely we need some sign that he is active in the world?

See also

3. The Indian and the ice
24. Squaring the circle
61 Mozzarella moon
78. Gambling on God

46. Amoebaesque

The press had given him the nickname 'worm man', but his friends knew him as Derek. Scientists had manipulated his DNA to mimic one of the most amazing features of the common or garden worm: the ability to regenerate lost tissue. And it had worked. When they chopped off his hand to test him out, a new one had regrown within a month.

Then it all went wrong. His body was slowly deteriorating. To save his life they had to transplant his brain into a new body. However, a major mistake during the operation severed his brain in two.

Fortunately, both halves fully regenerated and both were successfully transplanted into new bodies. The only problem was that both the men who now had one of the brains believed they were Derek. What is more, both had Derek's memories, mental skills and personality. This created problems for Derek's boyfriend, who couldn't tell them apart. It also led to the Dereks getting entangled in a legal battle to claim Derek's assets. But which was the real Derek? They couldn't both be him, could they?

Source: Section 89 of *Reasons and Persons* by Derek Parfit (Oxford University Press, 1984)

Like a good detective, before we start trying to account for what has happened, we should get the facts clear. Where once we had one Derek, now we have two. Call them right-Derek and left-

Derek, after the hemispheres of the original brain they grew from. Which, if either, is Derek?

They can't both be Derek, because since the split they have been two people, not one. If right-Derek died, for example, and left-Derek lived on, would Derek be dead or alive? Since one person cannot be both dead and alive, Derek couldn't be both right- and left-Derek.

Perhaps neither right- nor left-Derek is Derek. But this seems a strange solution. If, for example, the left hemisphere had been destroyed in the operation and only the right had fully regenerated, we would surely say that right-Derek was Derek. If the left hemisphere had also regenerated, however, suddenly right-Derek isn't Derek at all, even though he is exactly the same in both circumstances. How can a difference in something external to right-Derek stop him being Derek?

The only remaining possibility is that one or other of right- and left-Derek, and one only, is Derek. But since they have an equal claim to his identity, why should we pick one rather than the other? An ascription of identity cannot be arbitrary. So all three possibilities – both, either or neither – seem wrong. But one must be right: there are no other options.

If none of the possible answers to a question is adequate, perhaps we're just asking the wrong question. It's like demanding an answer to 'When did you stop beating your wife?' when the beatings never started.

In the case of the worm man, the problem is that we are asking a question about identity over time – a one-to-one relation – when the thing in question has a one-to-many relation over time. The logic of identity just doesn't fit. We should talk instead about succession or continuation. So, both right- and left-Derek are *continuers* of Derek, but we should not ask which, if either, *is* Derek.

So perhaps the question we should ask is if Derek *survived* his ordeal. It looks as though he did. If that is true, it seems that Derek achieved personal survival without personal identity. Of course, ordinary selves do not divide as Derek did. Nonetheless, his tale may still be instructive. For what it suggests is that what matters for our survival is not that identity over time is preserved, but that there is the right kind of continuity between us and our future selves. Then it becomes a question of what we want to see continue. Is it our bodies? Our brains? Our inner lives? Our souls?

See also

2. Beam me up . . .
11. The ship *Theseus*
30. Memories are made of this
38. I am a brain

47. Rabbit!

Professor Lapin and his assistant were very excited at the prospect of building a lexicon for a previously unknown language. They had only recently discovered the lost tribe of Leporidae and today they were to begin recording the meanings of the words in their language.

The first word to be defined was 'gavagai'. They had heard this word being used whenever a rabbit was present, so Lapin was about to write 'gavagai = rabbit'. But then his assistant interjected. For all they knew, couldn't 'gavagai' mean something else, such as 'undetached rabbit part' or 'Look! Rabbit!'? Perhaps the Leporidae thought of animals as existing in four dimensions, over time and space, and 'gavagai' referred only to the part of the rabbit present at the moment of observation? Or perhaps 'gavagai' were only observed rabbits and unseen rabbits had a different name?

The possibilities seemed fanciful, but Lapin had to admit that they were all consistent with what they had observed so far. But how could they know which one was correct? They could make more observations, but in order to rule out all the possibilities they would have to know more or less everything about the tribe, how they lived and the other words they used. But then how could they even begin their dictionary?

Source: *Word and Object* by W. V. O. Quine (MIT Press, 1960)

Anyone who speaks more than one language will be well aware of certain words that cannot be easily translated from one to another. The Spanish, for example, talk about the 'marcha' of a city or party. This is similar but not identical to the Irish word 'craic', which is also hard to translate exactly into English. The closest equivalent might be 'buzz' or 'good time feel' but to know what 'marcha' or 'craic' means you really have to get under the skin of the language and culture to which they belong.

Similarly, there is not one translation of the verb 'to be' in Spanish. Rather, there are two, 'ser' and 'estar', and which one you need to use depends on differences in the meaning of 'be' which the English lexicon does not reflect. And it is not enough to know that 'esposas' means 'wives' in Spanish to have a full command of the word. You also need to know that it means 'handcuffs', and have an awareness of the traditional Spanish machismo.

What the story of the 'gavagai' suggests is that all words are like 'craic', 'marcha', 'ser' and 'esposas' in that their meanings are tied intimately to the practices of a culture and the other words in the language. Whenever we translate a word into another language we lose these crucial contexts. Most of the time, we can get away with this, since the meanings are similar enough for us to be able to use the word and function in the community of speakers that use it. Hence if Lapin thinks of 'gavagai' as 'rabbit', he'll probably get on fine, even if there are subtle differences in meaning between the two. But to understand the true meaning of 'gavagai' he must focus on the language and community in which it is embedded, not his English concepts and practices.

Why does this matter? We are apt to think of words as functioning as a kind of label for ideas or objects, which enables people who speak different first languages to talk about the same things and have the same ideas. It's just that they use different words to do so. On this model, words have a one-to-one relation to their meanings or the things they refer to.

But if we take the 'gavagai' story seriously, we need to change this picture radically. Words do not stand in a one-to-one relation with things and ideas. Rather, words are interconnected with each other and the practices of their speakers. Meaning is 'holistic', in that you can never truly understand one word in isolation.

If we accept this, all sorts of strange consequences follow. For example, what does it mean for any statement to be true? We tend to think that 'the rabbit sat on the mat' is true just if there is a rabbit which sat on the mat. Truth is about a correspondence between a sentence and a state of affairs. But this simple relation is not possible if the meaning of a sentence depends on the language and culture in which it is embedded. Instead of a simple correspondence between sentence and facts, there is a complex web of relations between facts, sentence, the wider language and culture.

Does that mean truth is relative to language and culture? It would be too quick to jump to that conclusion, but from the starting point of meaning holism, it might well be possible to walk slowly to it.

See also

19. Bursting the soap bubble
23. The beetle in the box
74. Water, water, everywhere
85. The nowhere man

48. Evil genius

The critics all agreed. The cinematography was breathtaking, the acting first rate, the dialogue crisp, the pacing perfect and the original score both magnificent in its own right and used expertly in the service of the movie. But they also agreed that *De Puta Madre* was morally repulsive. The worldview it presented was one in which Hispanics are racially superior to other human beings, cruelty to the old is seen as necessary, and childless women are liable to be raped with impunity.

There the consensus ended. For some, the moral depravity of the film undermined what would otherwise be its strong claims to being a great work of art. For others, the medium and the message needed to be separated. The film was both a great work of cinematic art and a moral disgrace. We can admire it for its former qualities and loathe it for the latter.

The debate was more than academic, for so repugnant was the film's message that it would be banned, unless it could be argued that its artistic merits justified exemption from censorship. The director warned that a ban would be a catastrophe for free artistic expression. Was he right?

This imaginary controversy has many real-life counterparts. Perhaps most notably, people still vehemently disagree as to the merits of Leni Riefenstahl's *Triumph of the Will*, a documentary about the Nazi Nuremberg rallies, and *Olympia*, a record of the 1936 Munich Olympics that reinforces the myths of Aryan superiority. For some, Riefenstahl was a brilliant filmmaker who put her talent in the service of evil; for others, the films are artistic as well as moral failures.

Oscar Wilde described one extreme position on this general debate when he wrote, 'There is no such thing as a moral or an immoral book. Books are well written or badly written.' Wilde's claim was that art was autonomous from morality, and so to apply the standards of ethics to art was simply a mistake.

Most would not go so far. Many, however, would argue that you can separate out aesthetic from ethical judgements, and that we may admire something from the aesthetic viewpoint, but not from the ethical.

Agreeing to that, however, does not end the debate. It is one thing to say that the ethical and aesthetic can be separated, quite another to say that therefore we can just set aside our moral judgements. It would be perfectly consistent to argue that *De Puta Madre* is an artistic triumph and a moral disgrace, and that the demands of morality trump those of art. In that case, we might want to ban a film we nonetheless recognise as having great artistic merit.

At the other end of the spectrum from Wilde is the view that artistic and moral merit are intimately connected. Keats wrote that 'beauty is truth, truth beauty'. If that is so, then any work of art which presents a distorted picture of reality is an aesthetic as well as a creative failure. A morally repugnant yet brilliant work of art would be a contradiction in terms, and those who admired *De Puta Madre* would be plain mistaken.

When apparently intelligent people all disagree so strongly on fundamentals, it is easy to despair and retreat into a 'whatever works for you' relativism. But that option, if followed in this case, simply won't work. The person resisting calls for *De Puta Madre* to be banned can hardly say that the opinion of those who disagree is just as good as his own, for to do so would require admitting that what he thinks is unreasonable – banning the movie – is reasonable after all. In the same way, the person who accepts the legitimacy of those opposing the ban castrates the case for censorship.

If there is indeed truth on both sides of the fence, then there must be some shared common ground. Finding it, however, is far from easy.

See also

12. Picasso on the beach
37. Nature the artist
66. The forger
86. Art for art's sake

49. The hole in the sum of the parts

Barbara and Wally jumped into the taxi at Oxford station. 'We're in a hurry,' said Barbara. 'We've just done London and are heading to Stratford-upon-Avon this afternoon. So please could you just show us the university and then bring us back to the station.'

The taxi driver smiled to himself, set the meter running and looked forward to receiving a big fare.

He took them all round the city. He showed them the Ashmolean and Pitt Rivers museums, as well as the botanic gardens and the museums of natural history and the history of science. His tour took in not only the famous Bodleian library, but the lesser known Radcliffe, Sackler and Taylor libraries too. He showed them all thirty-nine colleges as well as the seven permanent private halls. When he finally pulled up at the station, the meter showed a fare of £64.30.

'Sir, you are a fraud!' protested Wally. 'You showed us the colleges, the libraries and the museums. But, damn you, we wanted to see the university!'

'But the university is the colleges, libraries and museums!' replied the indignant cabbie.

'You expect us to fall for that?' said Barbara. 'Just because we're American tourists doesn't mean we're stupid!'

Source: Chapter 1 of *The Concept of Mind* by Gilbert Ryle (Hutchinson, 1949)

The reputation American tourists have in Britain for being loud, brash and stupid is somewhat unfair. For one thing, how many Brits would like to be judged on the basis of how our holiday-makers behave on the Costa del Sol?

This vignette is not intended as an attack on Americans, but as a striking example of a form of fallacious thinking that even the smartest minds fall foul of. Barbara and Wally have made what the Oxford philosopher Gilbert Ryle called a category mistake. They have thought of Oxford University as though it were the same kind of thing as the colleges, libraries and museums which comprise it: an institution housed in a specific building. But the university is not that kind of thing at all. There is no one place or building which you can point to and say 'that is the university'. It is, as the taxi driver rightly said, the institution to which all those particular buildings and parts belong.

But that does not mean that the university is a ghostly presence that mysteriously unites all the colleges, libraries and other parts of it. To think that would be to make another category mistake. It is neither a single material nor immaterial thing. We should not be misled by language and assume that because it is a singular noun it is a singular object.

Ryle thought that the most common way of thinking about the mind made a similar category mistake. Again, we have a singular noun – the mind – and so we tend to think there must be a singular thing which the noun labels. If we think that, though, we end up with one of two absurdities. Either we conclude the mind is the brain, which is absurd, because brains have mass and volume, but thoughts have neither; or we conclude that the mind must be some immaterial entity, a ghost in the biological machine that is our body.

We can avoid the need to offer either of these implausible answers once we recognise that the mind is not a single object at all. To say something has a mind is to say it wants, desires, understands, thinks and so on. Because we do all these things we say we have minds. But that doesn't require us to identify any object as being the mind. This is no more mysterious than the claim that a university is that which has colleges, libraries and so on, even though there is no object which is the university.

It's a neat solution to an age-old problem. Whether or not it really does solve – or perhaps dissolve – the problem of mind, the concept of the category mistake is a useful guard against confusing features of language and features of the world.

See also

24. Squaring the circle
31. Just so
62. I think, therefore?
83. The golden rule

50. The good bribe

The Prime Minister liked to think of himself as a 'pretty straight kind of guy'. He genuinely despised corruption and sleaze in government and wanted to run a cleaner, more honest administration.

Something had happened, however, that presented him with a real dilemma. At a Downing Street reception, a businessman known for his lack of scruples, but who did not have a criminal or civil conviction against him, took the PM aside. Whispering conspiratorially into his ear, he said, 'Many people don't like me and don't respect the way I run my affairs. I don't give a damn about that. What does annoy me is that my reputation means I'll never be honoured by my country.

'Well,' he continued, 'I'm sure you and I can do something about that. I'm prepared to give £10 million to help provide clean water for hundreds of thousands of people in Africa, if you can guarantee me that I'll be knighted in the New Year's honours list. If not, then I'll just spend it all on myself.'

He slapped the PM on the back, said, 'Think it over,' and slipped back into the crowd. The Prime Minister knew this was a kind of bribe. But could it really be wrong to sell one of his country's highest honours when the reward would be so obviously for the good?

For those who like their morality clear-cut, there are two different ways of making this dilemma a no-brainer. Take a narrow utilitarian view, where the morally desirable outcome is that which benefits the largest number of people, and of course the Prime Minister should accept the bribe. The moral mathematics is simple: if he accepts, hundreds of thousands get their clean water, a rich man gets to be called 'sir' and the only price to be paid is the irritation of those who balk at the sight of a greedy quasi-criminal being honoured by the Queen.

If you start from principles of integrity and due process however, then it is equally obvious that the Prime Minister should resist. Affairs of state must be governed by due process. To allow titles and honours to be bought by the wealthy, even if the money they pay goes to a good cause, corrupts the principle that the state grants its favours in terms of merit and not ability to pay.

To gauge any sense of the difficulty in this dilemma you need to feel the force of both arguments. Due process and the rule of law are surely important for any democratic and open society, but if bending the rules has overwhelmingly good consequences and only minor bad ones, isn't it foolish or even immoral to stick rigidly to them?

The nub of the problem is a phenomenon known as moral self-indulgence. The Prime Minister is keen to run a clean government, and that means keeping himself free from any taint of corruption. But in this case, his desire not to get his own hands dirty might require sacrificing the welfare of the many thousands of Africans who would otherwise get clean water. The accusation is that the PM is more interested in keeping himself pure than he is in making the world a better place. His apparent desire to be moral is therefore actually immoral. It is an indulgence for which others will pay in disease and walking for miles to collect water.

The Prime Minister may be aware of this, however, but still have many reservations. For if he allows himself to think in this way, what other corruptions will follow? Why not lie to the electorate, if by doing so he can win their support for a just war they would otherwise oppose? Why not support oppressive regimes, if in the long run that will help regional stability and prevent even worse ones coming to power? If the net consequences are all that matter for politicians, how can he maintain his desire to be a straight, honest and incorrupt leader? Or is that whole idea simply a naive dream?

See also

7. When no one wins
79. A Clockwork Orange
83. The golden rule
91. No one gets hurt

51. Living in a vat

Ever since the accident, Brian had lived in a vat. His body was crushed, but quick work by the surgeons had managed to salvage his brain. This procedure was now carried out whenever possible, so that the brain could be put back into a body once a suitable donor had been found.

But because fewer brains than bodies terminally fail, the waiting list for new bodies had got intolerably long. To destroy the brains, however, was deemed ethically unacceptable. The solution came in the form of a remarkable supercomputer from China, Mai Trikks. Through electrodes attached to the brain, the computer could feed the brain stimuli which gave it the illusion that it was in a living body, inhabiting the real world.

In Brian's case, that meant he woke up one day in a hospital bed to be told about the accident and the successful body transplant. He then went on to live a normal life. All the time, however, he was really no more than his old brain, kept alive in a vat, wired up to a computer. Brian had no more or less reason to think he was living in the real world than you or I. How could he – or we – ever know differently?

Sources: The first meditation from *Meditations* by René Descartes (1641); chapter 1 of *Reason, Truth, and History* by Hilary Putnam (Cambridge University Press, 1982); *The Matrix*, directed by Larry and Andy Wachowski (1999); Nick Bostrum's Simulation argument, www.simulation-argument.com

The possibility that we are brains in vats provided the premise for the hit science fiction movie *The Matrix*. In that film, the hero, Neo, played by Keanu Reeves, was spared the indignity of having no body, but his situation was essentially the same as Brian's. He thought he was living in the real world when, in fact, his brain was simply being fed information to present that illusion. Really, he was in a pod, immersed in a kind of amniotic fluid.

The sceptical doubt that we might be victims of such a whole-scale illusion is much older. The allegory of Plato's cave is an early precursor, as are the systematic doubts of Descartes, who wondered if we could be dreaming or deceived by a powerful demon.

What is neat about the brain-in-a-vat idea, however, is its plausibility. It certainly seems to be scientifically possible, which makes it more credible than a spooky demon deceiver.

Indeed, a recent argument has even suggested that it is overwhelmingly probable that we are living in a virtual reality environment, not perhaps as brains in vats, but as artificially created intelligences. The argument is that, given time, we or another civilisation will almost certainly be able to create artificial intelligences and virtual-reality environments for them to live in. Further, because these simulated worlds do not require the huge amount of natural resources to keep them going that biological organisms do, there is almost no limit to how many such environments could be created. There could be the equivalent of an entire planet Earth 'living' in one desktop computer of the future.

If all this is possible, we have only to do the maths to see that it is probable we are in one such simulation. Let us say that over the whole course of human history, for every human being that ever lives, there are another nine that are the creation of computer simulations. Both the simulations and the humans would believe that they are biological organisms. But 90 per cent of them would be wrong. And since we cannot know if we are simulations or real beings, there is a 90 per cent chance that we are wrong to think we are the latter. In other words, it is much more probable that we are living in something like the Matrix than it is that we are walking the real Earth.

Most people sense something fishy about the argument. But maybe that is simply because its conclusion is too startling. The question we need to ask is not whether it sounds incredible, but whether there is anything wrong with its logic. And identifying its flaws is a very difficult, if not impossible, task.

See also

1. The evil demon
28. Nightmare scenario
62. I think, therefore?
98. The experience machine

52. More or less

Carol had decided to use a large slice of her substantial wealth to improve life in an impoverished village in southern Tanzania. However, since she had reservations about birth-control programmes, the development agency which she was working with had come up with two possible plans.

The first would involve no birth-control element. This would probably see the population of the village rise from 100 to 150 and the quality of life index, which measures subjective as well as objective factors, rise modestly from an average of 2.4 to 3.2.

The second plan did include a non-coercive birth-control programme. This would see the population remain stable at 100, but the average quality of life would rise to 4.0.

Given that only those with a quality of life ranked as 1.0 or lower consider their lives not to be worth living at all, the first plan would lead to there being more worthwhile lives than the second, whereas the second would result in fewer lives, but ones which were even more fulfilled. Which plan would make the best use of Carol's money?

Source: Part four of *Reasons and Persons* by Derek Parfit (Oxford University Press, 1984)

Carol's dilemma is not simply one of choosing between quality or quantity, for when we use things such as quality of life indices we are quantifying quality. That is just as complicated as it sounds.

What is Carol trying to achieve? There are three plausible answers. One is to increase the number of worthwhile lives. Another is to increase the total amount of quality of life. And the third is to create the conditions for the most worthwhile forms of life as possible.

Consider the first option. Clearly, if she goes with the no-birth-control plan, there will be more lives worth living as a result. But is this a desirable outcome? If we think it is, it seems we are led to an absurd conclusion. For since all lives other than the most wretched are worth living, that would mean we should always try to bring as many people into the world as possible, just as long as the quality of their lives doesn't fall below a minimum level. But would it really be a good thing if we trebled the population of Britain, for example, impoverishing it in the process, in order to bring more lives worth living into the world?

The second possible goal is to increase the total amount of quality of life. Again, the first plan achieves this. Although the maths can only approximate to the reality, we can see roughly how 150 lives each with a 3.2 quality of life rating scores a total of 480 'points', whereas 100 lives each with a 4.0 rating scores only 400. So there is more quality of life under the first plan.

But this too can lead to absurdity. For if we use this as the basis for our judgements, we would think it better to bring 1,000 people into the world with the prospect of a miserable 1.1 quality of life rating than 100 with the maximum rating of 10. (The rating system used here is fictitious.)

That leaves the third possibility: create the conditions for the most worthwhile and satisfying forms of human life possible, and don't worry about trying to maximise either the total number of people or total amount of quality of life. It's better to have fewer people genuinely content than many more barely satisfied.

Although that sounds like a reasonable conclusion, it has

implications in other areas of life and ethics which some find more disturbing. For once we start to say that there is no value in creating more life for its own sake, even if those lives would be worth living, potential lives, in the form of early foetuses, no longer have any special value. The fact that a foetus might become a human being with a worthwhile life is no reason to think we are morally obliged to do all we can to ensure it does so. Of course, many are perfectly happy to accept this conclusion. Those who aren't need to ask themselves why they aren't.

See also

20. Condemned to life
84. The pleasure principle
87. Fair inequality
98. The experience machine

53. Double trouble

'Doctor, you've got to help me. I'm in terrible pain and I know I'm dying. Put me out of my misery. Kill me swiftly and painlessly now. I can't go on any longer.'

'Let me get this straight,' replied Dr Hyde. 'Are you suggesting that I should, say, give you a very high dose of painkillers – 20mg of morphine sulphate perhaps – a dose so high that you would soon lose consciousness and shortly afterwards die?'

'Yes! Please be merciful,' said the patient.

'I'm afraid that's something I cannot do,' replied Dr Hyde. 'However, I can see that you are in pain, so here's something I can do. In order to relieve your pain, I would need to give you a very high dose of painkillers, say 20mg of morphine sulphate, a dose so high, however, that you would soon lose consciousness and shortly afterwards die. How does that sound?'

'Just like your first suggestion,' replied the puzzled patient.

'Oh, but there's every difference in the world!' replied the doctor. 'My first suggestion was that I killed you, the second that I relieved your pain. I'm no murderer and euthanasia is illegal in our country.'

'But either way I'm out of my misery,' protested the patient.

'Yes,' said the doctor. 'But only one way spares mine.'

Dr Hyde's explanation of the difference between his two remarkably similar suggestions can appear to be mere sophistry, an attempt to give the patient what he wants while remaining within the confines of the law. For in many countries, such as Britain, it is illegal to shorten the life of a patient deliberately, even if they are in great distress and request it. However, it is permitted to take actions to reduce pain, even if it can be foreseen that this will hasten death. Intention therefore becomes the key. The same action – injecting 20mg of morphine sulphate – with the same consequences, can be legal if the intention is to relieve pain and illegal if the intention is to kill.

This is not just a strange by-product of the law. Behind the distinction is a very old principle of morality with its roots in Catholic theology. The principle of double effect states that it can be morally acceptable to do something in order to bring about a good, even if you can foresee that will also bring about something bad, as long as the intention is the good and not the bad consequence. The key is that to foresee is not the same as to intend, and it is intent that counts.

The principle can get a bad press because it looks like a way of justifying awkward moral choices. But if it is taken seriously, it is not obviously a sophistical get-out clause. For instance, we tend to assume that in the case of Dr Hyde, he really wants to give the patient his wish and is just seeking a way around the law. But we need to take seriously the possibility that Dr Hyde does not want to kill his patient at all. Nevertheless, he will reluctantly follow a course of action in pursuit of the noble cause of reducing suffering, even though he can see it will also lead to death. The difference between foresight and intent might be very important for how Dr Hyde views his own conscience.

The nagging doubt remains, however, that we are as responsible for what we foresee as we are for what we intend. If I start shooting my rifle into a forest, aware that I could easily kill a passer-by, it is no defence to say that, since killing people is not my intention, I'm off the moral hook if I accidentally shoot someone. If the principle of double effect is to be defensible, it has to explain why it too rules out such blatantly reckless behaviour.

See also

15. Ordinary heroism
29. Life dependency
71. Life support
89. Kill and let die

54. The elusive I

Here's something you can try at home. Or on the bus, for that matter. You can do it with your eyes closed or open, in a quiet room or a noisy street. All you have to do is this: identify yourself.

I don't mean stand up and say your name. I mean catch hold of that which is you, rather than just the things that you do or experience. To do this, focus your attention on yourself. Try to locate in your own consciousness the 'I' that is you, the person who is feeling hot or cold, thinking your thoughts, hearing the sounds around you and so on. I'm not asking you to locate your feelings, sensations and thoughts, but the person, the self, who is having them.

It should be easy. After all, what is more certain in this world than that you exist? Even if everything around you is a dream or an illusion, you must exist to have the dream, to do the hallucinating. So if you turn your mind inwards and try to become aware only of yourself, it should not take long to find it. Go on. Have a go.

Any luck?

Source: Book I of *A Treatise on Human Nature* by David Hume (1739–40)

Admit it. You failed. You looked for the one thing that you always assumed was there and found nothing. What does that mean? That you don't exist?

Let's get clear about what you would have found. The

moment you became aware of anything it would have been something quite specific: a thought, a feeling, a sensation, a sound, a smell. But in no such case would you have been aware of *yourself* as such. You can describe each of the experiences you had, but not the you that had them.

But, you might protest, how could I not be aware that it was I having these experiences? For instance, it is true that when I looked at the book in front of me, what I was aware of was the book and not me. But in another sense I was aware that it was *me seeing the book*. It just isn't possible to detach myself from the experience, which is why there is no special awareness of I, only an awareness of what *I* am aware of. That is not to say, however, that the 'I' can be taken out of the equation.

That may sound convincing, but it won't do: the problem remains that this 'I' is a nothing. It is like the point of view from which a landscape is painted. In one sense, the point of view cannot be taken from the painting, for it is of a landscape from a particular perspective, without which the painting would not be what it is. But this point of view is not itself revealed in the painting. For all we know, the point of view is a grassy knoll, a parked car or a concrete office block.

The self which has the experiences can be seen in exactly the same way. It is true that, if I look at the book in front of me, I am aware not only that there is a visual experience, but that it is an experience from a certain point of view. But nothing about the nature of that point of view is revealed by the experience. The 'I' is thus still a nothing, a contentless centre around which experiences flutter like butterflies.

On this view, if we ask what the self is, the answer is that it is nothing more than the sum of all the experiences that are connected together by virtue of sharing this one point of view. The self is not a thing and it is certainly not knowable to itself. We have no awareness of what we are, only an awareness of what we experience. That doesn't mean we don't exist, but it does mean that we lack a constant core of being, a single self that endures over time, which we so often assume, wrongly, makes us the individuals we are.

See also

56. Total perspective vortex
62. I think, therefore?
65. Soul power
88. Total lack of recall

55. Sustainable development

The Green family realised that their success was exacting a high price. Their country farmhouse was their home as well as their business premises. But while their enterprise was creating a healthy profit, the vibrations caused by the heavy machinery used on site was slowly destroying the fabric of the building. If they carried on as they were, in five years the damage would make the building unsafe and they would be forced out. Nor were their profits sufficient to fund new premises or undertake the necessary repairs and structural improvements required.

Mr and Mrs Green were determined to preserve their home for their children. And so they decided to slow production and thus the spread of the damage.

Ten years later, the Greens passed away and the children inherited the family estate. The farmhouse, however, was falling to pieces. Builders came in, shook their heads and said it would cost £1 million to put right. The youngest of the Greens, who had been the accountant for the business for many years, grimaced and buried his head in his hands.

'If we had carried on at full production and not worried about the building, we would have had enough money to put this right five years ago. Now, after ten years of under-performance, we're broke.'

His parents had tried to protect his inheritance. In fact, they had destroyed it.

Source: *The Skeptical Environmentalist* by Bjorn Lomborg (Cambridge University Press, 2001)

This parable could be taken simply as a lesson about forward planning in business. But it is more interesting than that, for the tale can be seen as mirroring a serious dilemma of much wider concern: how do we respond to the environmental threats facing us today?

Take climate change. Experts agree that it is happening and that it is probably man-made. But there are no measures we can realistically take now that will stop it altogether. The Kyoto agreement, for example, would only delay it by about six years. However, the cost to the United States alone of implementing the agreement would be the equivalent of the money required to extend provision of clean drinking water to all the world's population. You have therefore to ask whether the cost of Kyoto is worth paying.

The point is not that, without Kyoto, the US would in fact provide clean water for all. The point is rather in the parallel to the Greens. Could we end up with a situation where we merely delay the inevitable at the cost of economic growth, thus depriving future generations of the funds they would need to sort out the problems they will inherit? It can't be better to postpone the problem of global warming if doing so merely leaves us less well equipped to confront it when it starts to hurt.

That is not to say that we should do nothing about global warming. It is merely to point out that we should make sure what we do is effective and doesn't inadvertently make things worse. That requires us to take into account more than just the spread of environmental damage, but future generations' ability to deal with it. A lot of green campaigners seek to avoid damage to the environment at all costs, but that is as shortsighted as the Greens' strategy of minimising damage to their farmhouse at all costs.

This would seem to be just common sense, but it is intuitively unappealing to those who care about the environment, for three reasons. First, it suggests it is sometimes better to let the Earth get more polluted in the short term. Second, it emphasises the role of economic growth in providing the source of solutions to problems. That emphasis on finance and economics is anathema to many greens. Third, it is often linked to the idea that future technologies will help bring solutions. And technology is seen by many environmentalists as a source of our problems, not their solution. Those three reasons might explain why Greens resist the argument, but not why they should.

See also

10. The veil of ignorance
22. The lifeboat
60. Do as I say, not as I do
87. Fair inequality

56. The total perspective vortex

Ian Ferrier had for years dreamed of building the total perspective vortex. But now, as he stood ready to test it out, he was questioning whether the whole endeavour was a terrible mistake.

The machine, which he had first come across as a piece of science fiction in a late twentieth-century radio programme, would enable whoever went into it to see their true place in the universe. The idea of the original fiction was that anyone who used the machine would find the fact of their own insignificance so crushing that it would destroy their very soul.

Ferrier had cheated a little in building the machine: everyone would see the same thing, since, he reasoned, we are all more or less as insignificant as each other. But throughout the project he had been convinced the machine would not crush his soul at all. He, like Camus's Sisyphus, condemned to push a boulder endlessly uphill only to see it roll back down again, would be able to confront the absurdity of his own insignificance and prevail.

And yet, now he was about to test it out, he did feel more than a little apprehensive. Could he really accept his own infinitesimal smallness in the grand scheme of things? There was only one way to find out . . .

Source: *The Restaurant at the End of the Universe* by Douglas Adams (Pan Books, 1980)

As a thought experiment, the total perspective vortex is contradictory. On the one hand, it invites us to imagine what would be the case if we entered the vortex, but on the other, the whole point of the hypothetical device is that we cannot imagine what it shows us.

Nevertheless, there is still some value in considering what effects the vortex might have. In *The Hitchhiker's Guide to the Galaxy*, the source of the vortex idea, one person does survive the experience. Zaphod Beeblebrox walks out calmly, saying the machine had showed him only what a 'terrific and great guy' he was. But we are left unsure whether Beeblebrox has really survived the machine or whether what he saw presented a distorted picture of his own significance.

Could he have survived the real thing? Well, why not? Consider what it means for anything to have value or significance. It is all a question of using the appropriate scale. What is significant in the context of a friendly game of golf matters not one jot to the international tour circuit. What happens at the US Open is insignificant in the context of the march of human history. And what happens on Earth is insignificant in the context of the whole universe. All this is true, but it does not show that the only true measure of something's significance or value is its impact on the universe as a whole. To judge your life in that way, and hence succumb to the vortex, is arguably just to measure your life against the wrong ruler.

Consider also how much depends on the eye of the beholder. Zaphod Beeblebrox has an enormous ego. Faced with the vortex, does he really see what others see? Where others despair at their infinitesimal smallness, does he not instead wonder at how important he is for his size?

That is where the vortex idea begins to lose coherence. It is supposed to show one's significance, but there are no facts of the matter to be shown. You can show someone's importance for a particular purpose, as the most-valuable-player rankings in American professional sport do. But there are any number of ways of determining our importance and there is no objective means of saying which one should count. Consider how people would give up fame and fortune just to be with one person whom they value and who values them. What does it matter to them that in the grand scheme of things their love counts for nought? To them, it counts for everything, and that is enough.

See also

20. Condemned to life
51. Living in a vat
54. The elusive I
62. I think, therefore?

57. Eating Tiddles

'Waste not, want not,' was Delia's motto. She had a great respect for the thriftiness of her parents' generation, people who had lived through the war and most of their lives with relatively little. She had learned a lot from them, skills virtually no one her age had, such as how to skin a rabbit and make tasty, simple dishes from offal.

So when she heard a scream of brakes one day outside her suburban semi in Hounslow, and went outside to find that Tiddles, the family cat, had been struck by a car, her first thoughts were not just of regret and sadness, but practicalities. The feline had been bashed but not run over. In effect, it was a lump of meat just waiting to be eaten.

The pungent meat stew her family sat down to that evening was of a kind not found on many British dining tables today, but Delia's family was used to eating cuts of meat that were no longer fashionable. She had told her husband what had happened, of course, and had always been direct with her children. Still, the youngest, Maisie, ate reluctantly and cast her mother occasional accusing glares over her steaming bowl. Delia was sympathetic, but the child surely had no reason to think she had done anything wrong.

Source: 'Affect, culture and morality, or is it wrong to eat your dog?' by Jonathan Haidt, Silvia Helena Koller and Maria G. Dias in the *Journal of Personality and Social Psychology*, 65 (1973)

The power of taboo is very strong. In the West, as in most of the world, most people eat meat with no moral qualms at all. Sometimes the flesh they dine on has been produced from animals kept in terrible conditions. Some farm animals, such as pigs, are more intelligent than many household pets.

Yet eating certain types of meat is seen as repulsive. Many Britons think eating horses or dogs is barbaric, whereas British Muslims think it is eating pigs which is repellent. And eating pets is considered particularly repugnant. Rabbit stew is perfectly acceptable, just as long as it isn't the rabbit you gave a name to and kept in a hutch.

Is there any moral basis to these judgements, or are they no more than culturally conditioned reflex reactions? Assuming you are not an ethical vegetarian, in which case all meat eating would be wrong, it is hard to see how morality comes into it. And in the case of Delia, it may be *more* moral to eat the family cat. After all, we do think there is something immoral about wilfully wasting resources when so many in the world are poor. So if eating meat is not wrong, and a source of meat becomes available, discarding it would seem to be wrong – not, eating it. On this account, Delia is a kind of moral hero, doing the good deed most others do not have the courage to.

It might be objected that to eat a pet is to betray the trust that the relationship with it was based on. You cannot just flip from being a friend and protector to pragmatic farmer. That is not only psychologically difficult, it also undermines the basis of the human–animal relationship.

It is not difficult to imagine, however, a culture where eating pets, or even friends, is seen as the logical culmination of that relationship. In Philip Pullman's *His Dark Materials* trilogy, the armoured bear, Iorek, honours his dead friend Lee Scoresby by eating him. Although most of the books' readers are children,

Pullman says that they seem to have no problem accepting the naturalness of this.

So perhaps the question of whether an animal is friend or food presents a false dichotomy. It is not only morally acceptable to eat our dead pets, it is culpably wasteful not to.

See also

5. The pig that wants to be eaten
17. The torture option
35. Last resort
91. No one gets hurt

58. Divine command

And the Lord spake unto the philosopher, 'I am the Lord thy God, and I command thee to sacrifice thy only son.'

The philosopher replied, 'There's something not right here. Your commandments say, "Thou shalt not kill".'

'The Lord giveth the rules and the Lord taketh away,' replied God.

'But how do I know you are God?' insisted the philosopher. 'Perhaps you are the devil trying to fool me?'

'You must have faith,' replied God.

'Faith – or insanity? Perhaps my mind is playing tricks? Or maybe you're testing me in a cunning way. You want to see if I have so little moral fibre that at the command of a deep voice booming through the clouds, I commit infanticide.'

'Me almighty!' exclaimed the Lord. 'What you're saying is that it is reasonable for you, a mere mortal, to refuse to do what I, the Lord thy God, commands.'

'I guess so,' said the philosopher, 'and you've given me no good reasons to change my mind.'

Source: *Fear and Trembling* by Søren Kierkegaard (1843)

In the book of Genesis, God found a more compliant servant in Abraham, who went along with the instruction to sacrifice his son, until the last minute, when, knife in hand, he was stopped from going ahead by an angel. Abraham has been presented as a paradigm of faith ever since.

What on earth was Abraham thinking? Let us assume that Abraham firmly believed in God and that God exists – this is not an atheist critique of his actions. Abraham then receives the instruction to kill his son. But wouldn't he be mad simply to go ahead and do so? All the problems raised by the philosopher in our version of the tale apply. It might not be God talking, but the devil; Abraham might be mad; the test might be to see if he refuses. All three of these possibilities seem more plausible than the idea that God wants his son dead, since what kind of loving God would command such a barbaric act?

In the book of Genesis, the human characters seem to have a much more direct relationship with their maker than believers do today. God talks to people like Abraham as though they were literally sitting side by side. In such a world, the identity of the being instructing the murder would not be in doubt. In the world we know, no one can be so sure that they have actually heard God's word. And even if they could, there is still some uncertainty as to whether the test is to see if Abraham would refuse.

So if this really is a story about the nature of faith, what is its message? It is not simply that a person of faith will do God's bidding, however unpleasant. It is that a person of faith can never know for sure what God's bidding is. Faith does not just enter the picture when action is called for; faith is required to believe in the first place, despite the lack of evidence. Indeed, faith sometimes needs the devout to go beyond the evidence and believe what is contrary to all they previously thought was right and true; for instance, that God does not approve of pointless killing.

This is not the faith that is often preached from the pulpits. That faith is a secure rock which provides the believer with a kind of calm, inner certainty. But if Abraham was prepared to kill his son serene in his own faith, then he couldn't have realised just what a risk he was taking with his leap of faith.

If you remain unpersuaded, consider for a moment the people who believe that God wishes them to become suicide bombers, to murder prostitutes or to persecute an ethnic minority. Before you say that God could never command such wicked things, remember that the God of the three Abrahamic faiths not only ordered the sacrifice of Isaac, but also condoned the rape of a wife as punishment to the husband (2 Samuel 12), ordered the killing of followers of other religions (Deuteronomy 13) and sentenced blasphemers to death by stoning (Leviticus 24). It seems there are no limits to what God might ask, and some people of faith will do.

See also

8. Good God
18. Rationality demands
34. Don't blame me
95. The problem of evil

59. The eyes have it

If you could view the world through other people's eyes, what would you see? This question had ceased to be either hypothetical or metaphorical for Cecilia. She had just tried out the remarkable U-View™ Universal Visual Information Exchange Web. This enables one person to connect themselves to another in such a way as to see exactly what that person sees, as she sees it.

This is a remarkable experience for anyone. But for Cecilia it was even more startling. For when she saw the world as her friend Luke did, it was as though the world had turned inside out. For Luke, tomatoes were the colour she knew as blue. The sky was red. Bananas turned from yellow to green when they ripened.

When the U-View people heard about Cecilia's experience they subjected her to further tests. It transpired that she saw the world with what they called an inverted spectrum: every colour looked to her like the complement of the colour it looked to other people. But of course, because the differences were systematic, if it weren't for the U-View system no one would ever have known. After all, she rightly called tomatoes red just like everyone else.

Could it be that you see the world as Cecilia does? If I could look through your eyes, would I think that, for you, the setting sun is blue? We cannot possibly know. For however you see the world, just as long as your sensory colour scheme is as regular as mine, nothing in what we say or do could ever reveal the differences. For both of us, green would be the colour of grass, lettuce, peas and the ink on a $1 note. Oranges would be orange, the angry would see red and singers get the blues.

The accuracy with which we use colour words is determined entirely by reference to public objects, not private experience. There is no way to get behind your eyes to see what blue really looks like to you. I just have to assume that, given our similar biologies, there is not much difference between how we both see a clear summer sky.

You might ask how it is then possible to know people are colour blind. The answer to that supports rather than weakens the case that the Cecilias of this world would live among us undetected. Colour blindness is revealed by the inability to discriminate between two colours that those with full colour vision perceive as clearly distinct. So, for example, red might fail to stand out against a green background, as it does for the majority. The tests that reveal this do not enter into the private experiences of sense experience. They simply determine people's ability to make public judgements about colour differences. So as long as someone is able to discriminate colour differences as well as everyone else, we would remain ignorant about any variations in how the colours actually look to them compared to us.

The fact that people might see the world in a different way to ourselves (or hear, smell, taste or feel it differently for that matter) is little more than an intriguing sceptical doubt. What is perhaps more interesting is what the possibility tells us about the use of language, and the meaning of words which describe our mental lives. In short, it seems a word like 'red' does not describe a particular visual sensation, but simply a regularity in the world that corresponds to a regularity in how we see it. When we say that a tomato is red, the word 'red' does not then refer to a colour we perceive, but to a feature of the world that may appear very differently to others. This means that when Cecilia and Luke both say that the sky is blue, both are correct, even though what they see is very different.

If this is true of colours, is it also true of other things we usually think of as inner and private? Is 'pain' a sensation or a kind of response to a sensation? Am I wrong to think that when I talk about my headache I am referring to the unpleasant sensation in my head? Does this turn the language of the mind inside out?

See also

13. Black, white and red all over
21. Land of the Epiphens
41. Getting the blues
73. Being a bat

60. Do as I say, not as I do

Irena Janus was preparing her presentation on the impact of flying on global warming. She would tell her audience that commercial flights pump more of the major greenhouse gas CO_2 into the atmosphere in one year than all of Africa does. She would tell them how one long-haul flight is more polluting than twelve months of car travel. If we want to save the Earth, she would conclude, we must do more to reduce the number of flights we take and encourage people to either travel less or use other forms of transport.

Just as she was imagining the rapturous reception her talk would receive, she was interrupted by the air stewardess offering her some wine. Hypocrisy? Not as Janus saw it. For she also knew full well that the impact of her own flights on the environment was negligible. If she refused to fly, global warming would not be delayed by as much as a second. What was needed was mass change and policy change. Her work, which involved flying around the world advocating this, could thus be part of the solution. Refusing to fly would simply be a hollow gesture.

And with that she switched on the in-flight movie: *The Day After Tomorrow*.

It is comforting to think that 'every little helps', but is it true? It depends on how you look at it. For example, if everyone in Britain gave £1 to a charity appeal, together they would raise

£56 million. Nobody would have done much individually, but collectively they would have raised a huge amount. But on the other hand, if all but one person donates and the total sum raised is £55,999,999, the extra pound that this last person withholds wouldn't make any significant difference to what could be done with the money.

Reflecting on these facts, it is perfectly rational to conclude that my own contribution is insignificant and so it doesn't matter if I make it or not, but also that it really would matter if everyone reasoned the same way. Is that a paradox, or can the two thoughts be reconciled?

Janus thinks they can. What you have to do is persuade a large number of people that their contributions do matter. If enough of them wrongly believe this to be true, then we get the favourable impact we desire. What this amounts to is a programme of honourable deception. The collective effort works, not the individual one. But unless people think the individual effort matters, you won't be able to muster the collective one.

There is something profoundly unpersuasive about this line of reasoning, but it is hard to fault the logic. Why, then, do we feel it is wrong?

One possible reason is that, despite Janus's salved conscience, we feel she is a hypocrite, for she does the opposite of what she asks us to do. But this does not show her reasoning about the impact of individual endeavours is wrong. Her justification for flying might be perfectly rational, if she is concerned only with saving the planet. Her choosing to fly could still be wrong, however, for an entirely different reason, namely that it is wrong to do what you tell others they should not do. In other words, the reason it is wrong for her to fly has nothing to do with the environment and everything to do with the ethical imperative to apply the same rules to your own conduct as you do to others.

This seems to resolve the apparent paradox. It is true that collectively our fondness for flying is harmful: all the little emissions add up. It is also true that individual flights have a negligible impact: no individual little emission matters. But it is also true that if we advocate a policy of reducing emissions, we cannot make exceptions for ourselves. Janus should not be criticised for destroying the planet but for not following the advice she gives others. Unless, of course, do as I say and not as I do is a perfectly reasonable request.

See also

55. Sustainable development
82. The freeloader
83. The golden rule
91. No one gets hurt

61. Mozzarella moon

The moon is made of cheese – mozzarella, to be precise. By saying that, I may have signed my own death warrant. You see, they don't want us to know. They'll claim I'm mad. But as Kurosawa said, 'In a mad world, only the mad are sane.'

'But men have walked on the moon,' you say. Wrong. It was all a fake, filmed in a studio by NASA. Haven't you seen the movie *Capricorn One*? If it weren't for lawyers, that would have been billed as a documentary.

'But other non-manned trips have been made to the moon.' Most of them were fakes too. Some weren't, and those were the ones that brought back samples proving the mozzarella theory. But of course, the evidence has been suppressed.

'But people can look at the moon through telescopes.' Right, and you're telling me that you can tell from that whether the moon is hard rock or soft cheese?

'But if this were true, surely it would have got out.' Would you keep quiet, perhaps getting paid off handsomely; or be killed or discredited as a madman?

Think about it: how else would Elvis be able to stay alive up there if he didn't have an endless supply of cheese?

Crazy, isn't it? But what about the 20 per cent of Americans who believe the moon landings never took place? Are they all crazy too? If not, what makes theirs a sane, even if mistaken, belief to hold and the mozzarella moon hypothesis incredible hokum?

Conspiracy theories are made possible because of two limitations of knowledge formation. The first is what could be called the holistic nature of understanding: any single thing we believe is connected, web-like, to any number of other beliefs. So, for example, your belief that ice cream is fattening is connected to your beliefs about the calorific content of ice cream, the connection between fat consumption and weight-gain, the reliability of nutritional science and so on.

The second is what is rather grandly called the underdetermination of theory by evidence. In plain English that means that the facts never provide enough evidence to conclusively prove one theory and one theory only. There is always a gap – the possibility that an alternative theory is true. That is why courts insist on proof only beyond 'reasonable doubt'. Proof beyond *all* doubt is impossible.

Put these two limitations together and space opens up for even the wildest of conspiracy theories. There is overwhelming evidence that the moon is a lump of rock, but we are not *compelled* by the evidence to reach this conclusion. The evidential gaps mean that the evidence can be made consistent even with the hypothesis that the moon is made of cheese. All we need to do is rearrange all the other interconnected beliefs we have in our web of understanding so that they too fit. Hence the need to reassess the power of microscopes, the extent of corruption, and the veracity of the moon landings.

For sure, what you end up with can sound pretty wild. But the crucial point is that it *fits the evidence*. This is what makes so many people fall under the spell of conspiracy theories (and other outlandish ideas about the nature of the universe). The fact that 'it all fits' seems to be a compelling reason for belief. But any number of different theories fit, including the notion that the moon is made of cheese.

So what makes one theory better than another? Why is the theory of evolution sound and the theory that the moon landings were staged absurd? There's no easy answer to that, which perhaps in part explains why nearly half of all Americans think that the theory of evolution is bunkum too. All we can say is that mere consistency with the evidence is not enough to make a theory rationally compelling. If you believe that, then you may as well accept that Elvis is orbiting us right now, in pizza-topping heaven.

See also

1. The evil demon
3. The Indian and the ice
19. Bursting the soap bubble
98. The experience machine

62. I think, therefore?

My name is René. I remember reading once that if there is one thing I can always be certain of, it's that as long as I'm thinking, I exist. If I, David, am thinking right now, I must exist in order for the thinking to go on. That's right, isn't it? I may be dreaming or I may be mad, or maybe I don't live in Taunton at all, but as long as I'm thinking I know that Lucy (that's me) exists. I find this comforting. My life in Munich can be very stressful, and knowing that I can be certain of the existence of my self provides some security. Walking down the Champs-Elysées every morning, I often find myself wondering if the real world exists. Do I really live in Charlottesville, as I think? Friends say to me, 'Madeleine, you will drive yourself mad with your speculations!' But I don't think I'm nuts. I've found certainty in an uncertain world. *Cogito ergo sum*. I, Nigel, think, therefore I am indeed Cedric.

Sources: Discourse on Method by René Descartes (1637), *Schriften und Briefe* by G. C. Lichtenberg (Carl Hanser Verlag, 1971)

Is this monologue coherent? In one sense it clearly is not. The speaker keeps changing his or her name, and makes conflicting claims about where s/he lives. Superficially it's a mess.

However, in one important sense it is completely coherent. More specifically, it is entirely consistent with the truth of 'I think, therefore I am'. René Descartes, who first wrote that, took it to establish the existence of an immaterial soul or self. But critics have argued that in doing so he claimed more than his argument had proved. Our bizarre monologue shows why.

The key point is that the certainty you get from 'I think, therefore I am' comes only in the moment of its thinking. It is indeed true that in order for there to be a thought, there must indeed be a thinker to have it. But that momentary certainty does not demonstrate that the same thinker exists over time, or is the same one who had a thought a few minutes ago. Indeed, it is consistent with the thinker popping into existence only for the time it takes to have the thought.

This is how to make sense of the monologue. These are not the words of a single, continuous self, but a series of thoughts by a sequence of selves, all of whom take turns to occupy the position of the speaker. We do not need to think of this in occult terms. Think rather of someone with an acute multiple personality disorder. The different personae take it turns, in rapid succession, to control the voice function. At the time each of them says 'I think, therefore I am' what they say is absolutely true. It is just that it is no sooner said than the 'I', whose existence was so incontrovertible, disappears. Perhaps we could even have the situation portrayed by the last sentence, in which a second 'I' completes the thought of the first.

Given that most of us do not have multiple personalities, what is the significance of this for us? The point of the monologue is to show that Descartes's famous words demonstrate a great deal less than we often take them to. The fact that we think may show that we exist, but it does not tell us anything about what kind of thing we are, or whether we continue to exist as the same person over time. The certainty we get from *cogito ergo sum* comes at a high price: complete uncertainty once we step outside the moment in which the thought occurs.

See also

3. The Indian and the ice
28. Nightmare scenario
51. Living in a vat
54. The elusive I

63. No know

It was a very strange coincidence. One day last week, while Naomi was paying for her coffee, the man behind her, fumbling in his pockets, dropped his key ring. Naomi picked it up and couldn't help but notice the small white rabbit dangling from it. As she handed it back to the man, who had a very distinctive, angular, ashen face, he looked a little embarrassed and said, 'I take it everywhere. Sentimental reasons.' He blushed and they said no more.

The very next day she was about to cross the road when she heard a screeching of brakes and then an ominous thud. Almost without thinking, she was drawn with the crowd to the scene of the accident, like iron filings collecting around a magnet. She looked to see who the victim was and saw that same white, jagged face. A doctor was already examining him. 'He's dead.'

She was required to give a statement to the police. 'All I know is that he bought a coffee at that café yesterday and that he always carried a key ring with a white rabbit.' The police were able to confirm that both facts were true.

Five days later Naomi almost screamed out loud when, queuing once more for her coffee, she turned to see what looked like the same man standing behind her. He registered her shock but did not seem surprised by it. 'You thought I was my twin brother, right?' he asked. Naomi nodded. 'You're not the first to react like that since the accident. It doesn't help that we both come to the same café, but not usually together.'

As he spoke, Naomi couldn't help staring at what was in his hands: a white rabbit on a key ring. The man was not taken aback by that either.'You know mothers.They like to treat their kids the same.'

Naomi found the whole experience disconcerting. But the question that bothered her when she finally calmed down was: had she told the police the truth?

Source: 'Is Justified True Belief Knowledge?' by Edmund Gettier, republished in *Analytic Philosophy: An Anthology*, edited by A. P. Martinich and D. Sosa (Blackwell, 2001)

What Naomi said to the police was, 'All I know is that he bought a coffee at that café yesterday and that he always carried a key ring with a white rabbit.' Both facts turned out to be true. But was she right to say she *knew* them to be true?

Many philosophers have argued that knowledge has three conditions. To know something, you must first believe it to be true. You can't *know* that Rome is the capital of Italy if you *believe* Milan is. Second, what you believe must be true. You can't know Milan is the capital of Italy if Rome is. Third, your true belief must be justified in some way. If you just happen for no good reason, to believe that Rome is the capital of Italy, and it turns out you are right, we should not say you had knowledge; it was just a lucky guess.

Naomi had two true beliefs about the dead man. And she seemed justified in holding them. But it seems she really didn't know they were true. She did not know the man had a twin brother, who carried an identical key ring. So had the dead man been the twin of the man she had seen in the café, and had he neither visited the café the day before nor carried the same key ring, she would still have claimed to have known the same two things about him, only this time she would have been wrong.

To get some idea of how little she actually knew, even now she does not know whether the man she saw in the café the day before the accident was the twin who died in the accident or the one whom she saw in the café days later. She has no idea which is which.

The obvious solution to this problem seems to be that we need to tighten up the idea of justification. Naomi didn't know because her justification for claiming to know the two facts about the dead man was not strong enough. But if this is true, then we need to demand that knowledge has very strict conditions for justification of belief across the board. And that means we will find that almost all of what we think we know is not sufficiently justified to count as knowledge. If Naomi really didn't know what she thought she knew about the dead man, then we don't really know much of what we think we know either.

See also

1. The evil demon
3. The Indian and the ice
40. The rocking-horse winner
76. Net head

64. Nipping the bud

The president lowered his voice and said, 'What you are suggesting is illegal.'

'Yes indeed, Mr President,' replied the general. 'But you have to ask yourself how best to protect the lives of your citizens. The situation is simple: Tatum is determined both to mount a campaign of ethnic cleansing in his own country and to launch military attacks on us. Our intelligence tells us that he is almost alone in this view and that if we were to take him out, he would be replaced by the far more moderate Nesta.'

'Yes, but you talk about us taking him out. Assassination of a foreign leader is contrary to international law.'

The general sighed. 'But Mr President, you must see how simple your choice is. One bullet, followed by a few more as security services clean up afterwards, will be enough to avert a widespread massacre and probable war. I know you don't want the blood of a foreign leader on your hands, but would you prefer to be drowning in the blood of thousands of his, and your own, people?'

Morality is a higher authority than the law. That is why we approve of civil disobedience when the state's laws are manifestly unjust and there are no legal ways to oppose them. We might disagree as to what particular actions were justified in the African National Congress's struggle against apartheid, but the idea that

South Africa provided ample opportunities for legal protests by the country's blacks is ludicrous.

It is not difficult to imagine situations where law-breaking is the right thing to do. It is more important to save life than honour speed limits. You should not give up the pursuit of a dangerous criminal in order to avoid trespassing. It is better to steal than starve to death.

If we accept that, then the mere fact that what our President is being asked to do is contrary to international law does not settle the question of whether he should go ahead. The question is rather, are the circumstances so serious that there is no way to avoid a terrible outcome without resorting to illegal acts?

If the calculations presented by the general are correct, then it would seem that the assassination would be justified. As the well-worn example runs, if you knew what Hitler would go on to do, would you have killed him in his youth? If not, why do you value his life over those of the six million killed in the Holocaust and countless others in his wars?

However, as the overthrow of Saddam Hussein showed, the problem is that intelligence is far from infallible. The fact is that, although in hindsight we might wish we had acted earlier, we can never know for sure what the future will bring. Assassination might prevent ethnic cleansing and war. On the other hand, it might provoke greater unrest, or simply leave someone else to command the killing. The law of unintended consequences needs to be respected.

But the President cannot afford the luxury of shrugging his shoulders and saying '*que será, será*'. The politician's job is to make decisions based on the best possible estimation of present and future circumstances. The fact that estimates can be wrong is no excuse for inaction. Decisions are never made on the basis of absolute certainty but probability.

So the dilemma remains. If Tatum is not assassinated and he goes on to do what is predicted, it would be a weak defence for the President to say, 'Yes, I knew that was probable but I couldn't be sure, so I sat on my hands.' At the same time, he cannot flout international laws regularly on the basis of potentially unreliable information. How then does he reach his decision in this particular case? With great difficulty, for sure.

See also

9. Bigger Brother
36. Pre-emptive justice
50. The good bribe
77. The scapegoat

65. Soul power

Faith had believed in reincarnation for as long as she could remember. But recently her interest in her past lives had reached a new level. Now that she was visiting the medium mystic Marjorie, for the first time she had information about what her past lives were really like.

Most of what Marjorie told her was about her previous incarnation as Zosime, a noblewoman who lived at the time of the siege of Troy. She heard about her daring escape first to Smyrna and then on to Knossos. She was apparently both brave and beautiful, and she fell in love with a Spartan commander, whom she lived with at Knossos for the rest of her life.

Faith didn't check the real history of Troy to try to verify Marjorie's story. She did not doubt that hers was the same soul that had lived in Zosime. She did, however, have a nagging concern about what this all meant. Much as she enjoyed the idea of being a Greek beauty, since she didn't remember anything of her life in Knossos or have any sense of being the person Marjorie told her about, she couldn't see how she and Zosime could be the same person. She had found out about her past life, but it didn't seem like *her* life at all.

Source: Book two, chapter XXVII of *An Essay Concerning Human Understanding* by John Locke (5th edn, 1706)

Many people all over the world believe in various forms of reincarnation or rebirth. There are plenty of reasons for thinking that they are mistaken to do so. Let us suppose, though, that we do have souls and these are reincarnated. What would follow from that?

This is the question Faith is grappling with. Despite the somewhat suspicious nature of the story Marjorie told her – why is it our past lives always seem to be as interesting, powerful people with colourful lives? – Faith does not dispute its veracity. The question she asks is: if I do indeed have the same soul as Zosime, does that make me the same person as her?

Faith intuitively answers 'no'. She has no sense of being the same person as Zosime. This is not surprising. When we look back at ourselves in the past (rather than at our past selves), what gives us a sense that we are the same person is a certain degree of psychological connectedness and continuity. We remember being that person, doing the things she did, holding the beliefs she held and so on. We also have a sense of how our current selves grew from that person.

If our souls did inhabit other persons in previous lives, we have no such psychological connections with them. Marjorie needs to tell Faith what Zosime did and thought, as Faith does not remember being Zosime; nor has she any sense of having grown out of Zosime. Without these connections, how can it make sense to talk about Zosime and Faith being the same person, even if they do share the same soul?

If these thoughts are on the right track, then even if we have souls that survive bodily death, this does not necessarily mean that *we* will survive bodily death. The continued existence of the self seems to depend on psychological continuity, not some strange immaterial substance. The continued existence of the soul no more guarantees the continued existence of the self than the continued existence of a heart or other organ does.

But now consider what it is like to look at a photograph of yourself as an infant. To know what that person was like, you usually have to ask someone who was an adult at the time and who remembers. 'What was I like?' you ask them, as Faith asks Marjorie, 'What was I like at Troy?' Your psychological links with that toddler may be so weak as to be almost non-existent. Does that mean you are, in a very real sense, no more the same person as your baby self than Faith is the same as Zosime?

See also

2. Beam me up . . .
38. I am a brain
54. The elusive I
88. Total lack of recall

66. The forger

Avenue of Poplars at Dawn was set to join the ranks of van Gogh masterpieces. This 'lost' work would sell for millions and generate volumes of scholarship comparing it to the two other paintings van Gogh made of the same scene at different times.

This pleased Joris van den Berg, for he, not van Gogh, had painted *Avenue of Poplars at Dawn*. Joris was an expert forger and he was certain that his latest creation would be authenticated as genuine. That would not only increase his wealth enormously but also give him tremendous professional satisfaction.

Only a few close friends knew what Joris was up to. One expressed very serious moral misgivings, which Joris had brushed off. As far as he was concerned, if this painting was judged to be as good as a van Gogh original, then it was worth every penny that was paid for it. Anyone who paid more than it was really worth *just because* it was van Gogh's own work was a fool who deserved to be parted from his money.

It may seem obvious that forgery is a less than virtuous profession, because it inevitably involves deceit. The forger succeeds only if he can mislead people as to the provenance of his work.

Deceit, however, is not always to be decried. Indeed, sometimes a barefaced lie can be just what morality demands. If a racist thug, intent on violence, asks you if you know where any 'foreigners' live, you would do best to profess ignorance, rather than direct them to number 23. What seems to matter, therefore, is whether the lie serves a noble or base purpose, and what the wider consequences of the deception are.

The forger's purpose seems to be less than pure: making lots of money for himself. However, even a bona fide artist can be at least part motivated by the desire to earn money, so this in itself doesn't settle matters. We need to look at the broader picture if we are to assess the art of forgery.

The imaginary tale of Joris van den Berg suggests a creditable way to defend his work. To put it in rather elevated terms, the forger is actually providing a service in reminding us of the true value of art and mocking the way in which the art market replaces aesthetic values with financial ones. The key point here is that the forger can succeed in one of two ways: he can produce a work which is as good as that of the master he is copying; or he can produce a work which is considered valuable simply because it is thought to be the work of a famous artist. If the fake is indeed as good as the work of the established artist, why shouldn't it be valued accordingly? If the fake isn't as good, we need to ask why people pay so much for inferior goods. Could it be because prices on the art market are not determined by aesthetic merit but by fashion, reputation and celebrity? The signature of van Gogh on a work adds value in the same way that the moniker of David Beckham adds value to a football shirt. If this is the truth, then it is rich to protest that such a shoddy trade can in any way be made less pure by the work of a forger.

In this light, the forger can be seen as a kind of guerrilla artist, fighting for the true values of creativity in a culture where art has been debased and commodified. It is true that he is a deceiver. But no guerrilla war can be waged in the open. The system has to be picked apart from within, piece by piece. And the war will be won only when every work of art is judged on its own merits, not on the basis of the signature in the corner. That is, unless anyone can provide good reasons for believing that the signature really does matter . . .

See also

12. Picasso on the beach
37. Nature the artist
48. Evil genius
86. Art for art's sake

67. The poppadom paradox

As life-transforming events go, the arrival of poppadoms at the table hardly counts as the most dramatic. But it gave Saskia the kind of mental jolt that would profoundly alter the way she thought.

The problem was that the waiter who delivered the poppadoms was not of Indian descent, but was a white Anglo-Saxon. This bothered Saskia because, for her, one of the pleasures of going out for a curry was the feeling that you were tasting a foreign culture. Had the waiter served her a steak and kidney pie it would have been no more incongruous than his skin colour.

The more she thought about it, however, the less sense it made. Saskia thought of herself as a multiculturalist. That is to say, she positively enjoyed the variety of cultures an ethnically diverse society sustains. But her enjoyment depended upon other people remaining ethnically distinct. She could enjoy a life flitting between many different cultures only if others remained firmly rooted in one. For her to be a multiculturalist, others needed to be monoculturalists. Where did that leave her ideal of a multicultural society?

Saskia is right to feel uncomfortable. There is a problem at the heart of liberal multiculturalism. It advocates respect for other cultures, but what it values above all is the ability to transcend one culture and value many. This places a major constraint on the extent of its respect. The ideal person is the multiculturalist who can visit a mosque, read Hindu scriptures and practise Buddhist meditation. Those who remain within one tradition do not embody these ideals, and so, despite the talk of 'respect', they can be seen only as inferior to the open-minded multiculturalist.

There is something of the zoo mentality in this. The multiculturalist wants to go around admiring different ways of living, but can do this only if various forms of life are kept more or less intact. Different subcultures in society are thus like cages, and if too many people move in or out of them, they become less interesting for the multiculturalist to point and smile at. If everyone were as culturally promiscuous as they were, there would be less genuine diversity to revel in. And so the multiculturalists must remain an elite, parasitic on internally homogenous monocultures.

It may be argued that it is possible to be both a multiculturalist and committed to one particular culture. The paradigm here is of the devout Muslim or Christian who nonetheless has a profound respect for other religions and belief systems and is always prepared to learn from them.

However, tolerance and respect for other cultures are not the same as valuing all cultures more or less equally. For the multiculturalist, the best point of view is the one which sees merit in all. But one cannot be a committed Christian, Muslim, Jew or even atheist and sincerely believe this. There may be tolerance, or even respect, for other cultures, but if a Christian really believed that Islam is as valuable as Christianity, why would they be a Christian?

This is the multiculturalist's dilemma. You can have a society of many cultures which respect each other. Call that multiculturalism if you want. But if you want to champion a multiculturalism which values diversity itself and sees all cultures as of equal merit, then you either have to accept that those who live within just one culture have an inferior form of life – which seems to go against the idea of respect for all cultures – or you have to argue for erosion of divisions between distinct cultures, so that people value more and more in the cultures of others – which will lead to a decrease in the kind of diversity you claim to value.

In our concrete example, for Saskia to continue to enjoy a diversity of cultures, she must hope that others do not embrace multiculturalism as fully as she has.

See also

10. The veil of ignorance
55. Sustainable development
82. The freeloader
84. The pleasure principle

68. Mad pain

The accident left David with a very unusual form of brain damage. If you scratched, pricked or kicked him, he felt no pain. But if he saw a lot of yellow, tasted oak, heard an opera singer hit a high C, made an unintentional pun, or had one of several other apparently random experiences, then he would feel pain, sometimes quite acutely.

Not only that, but he did not find the sensation of this pain at all unpleasant. He didn't deliberately seek out pain, but he did not make any efforts to avoid it either. This meant that he did not manifest his pain in the usual ways, such as crying out or writhing. The only physical signs of David being in pain were all forms of involuntary spasm: his shoulders would shrug, eyebrows lower and rise in quick succession, or his elbows flap out, making him look like a chicken.

David's neurologist, however, was deeply sceptical. He could see that David no longer felt pain as he had before, but whatever David was now feeling when he saw 'too much yellow', it couldn't be pain. Pain was by definition an unpleasant thing that people tried to avoid. Perhaps his brain damage had made him forget what the sensation of real pain felt like.

Source: 'Mad Pain and Martian Pain' by David Lewis, in *Readings in Philosophy of Psychology*, vol. 1, edited by Ned Block (Harvard University Press, 1980)

Philosophers of mind are keen on pain. They are fascinated by the nature of subjective experience and its relation to objective knowledge, and nothing seems to be more subjective and at the same time as real as pain. Just ask anyone who has suffered extreme toothache. At the same time, we are usually pretty good at spotting if someone is in pain. Unlike other mental events, such as thinking about penguins, pain affects our outer demeanour as well as our inner experience.

So if you want to understand what it means to have a subjective experience, pain makes for a good case study. The story of David's 'mad pain' is an attempt to play with the variables associated with pain to see which are essential and which are incidental. The three main variables are private, subjective experiences; typical causes; and behavioural responses. Mad pain has only subjective experience in common with ordinary pain; its causes and effects are quite different. If it is nonetheless accurate to describe mad pain as pain, then we should conclude that it is the subjective feeling of being in pain which is the essence of pain. Its causes and effects are merely incidental, and could be different from what they usually are.

Common sense is not univocal on this. On the one hand, it seems obvious to say that pain is essentially a subjective feeling. Only philosophers and psychologists would seriously suggest that it might be better defined in terms of stimulus-response or brain function. But on the other hand, common sense would also say that a subjective experience of pain which someone didn't mind having and which caused no agitation would not be pain at all. That means the story of David is incoherent: despite what he says, he just couldn't be feeling pain at all. His neurologist is right to be sceptical. And after all, we only have David's word to go on. Why should we trust his ability to recognise his inner sensations as being the same as those he had when he hurt himself before the accident?

The nub of the issue, however, concerns the relation between the inner and the outer. It might seem easy to say that pain is defined by how it feels to the sufferer, and that this has an essential link to behaviours such as avoidance and grimacing. But this solution is too quick. For if pain really is a feeling, then why should it be inconceivable to experience pain without any of the associated behaviour? It's no good just saying it *must* manifest itself in some way; you need to say *why* it must do so. Until you can, mad pain remains a possibility.

See also

23. The beetle in the box
26. Pain's remains
32. Free Simone
39. The Chinese room

69. The horror

'The horror! The horror!'

Many have speculated about what inspired Colonel Kurtz to utter those famous last words. The answer lies in what he realised just before he let out his last breath. In that moment, he understood that past, present and future were all illusions. No moment in time is ever lost. Everything that happens exists for ever.

That meant his impending death would not be the end. His life, once lived, would always exist. And so, in a sense, the life he had lived would be lived again and again, eternally recurring, each time exactly the same and thus with no hope of learning, of changing, of righting past wrongs.

Had Kurtz made a success of his life he could have borne that realisation. He could have looked upon his work, thought 'it is good' and gone to his grave serene in his triumph over death. The fact that he instead reacted with horror testified to his failure to overcome the challenges of mortal existence.

'The horror! The horror!' Would you react to the thought of eternal recurrence any differently?

Sources: *Thus Spake Zarathustra* by Friedrich Nietzsche (1891); *Heart of Darkness* by Joseph Conrad (1902)

As literary criticism and as metaphysics, this interpretation of Kurtz's dying words, from Joseph Conrad's *Heart of Darkness*, is at best complete speculation and at worst pure invention. I am not aware of any textual evidence that this is how we should understand Kurtz's enigmatic last words. And the idea of eternal recurrence, although seemingly believed in earnest by Nietzsche, is not considered by most commentators to have marked his finest hour.

Nonetheless, the hypothesis of eternal recurrence and how we would react to it is an interesting device for examining ourselves. Even if our lives are not fated to be infinitely repeated, whether or not we can bear the thought that they would be is, for Nietzsche, a test of whether we have 'overcome' life. Only the 'overman', who has complete self-mastery and control over his fate, could look upon his life with enough satisfaction to accept its eternal recurrence.

It is important to remember that what Nietzsche is talking about is not a kind of *Groundhog Day*. In that film, Bill Murray found himself in the same day again and again, but each time he had the opportunity to do things differently. Hence he had the possibility of redemption, of escaping the cycle, by finally learning how to love. Nietzsche's form of recurrence is one in which there is no awareness that one is doing the same thing again, and there is no opportunity to do it differently. It is literally the exact same life, lived again and again.

Nietzsche may have gone too far when he suggested that only the overman, who has never existed, could accept this. Indeed, it is interesting how many people, even those who have gone through hell, say, 'If I could go back, I would do all the same things again. I wouldn't change a thing.' On the face of it, that directly contradicts Nietzsche's claim about the intolerability of eternal recurrence. Perhaps it is not Nietzsche who is wrong, however, but those who blithely embrace their past mistakes. For when we truly try to imagine the bad experiences of our pasts, the terrible mistakes we made, the hurtful things we did, the indignities we suffered, isn't it unbearably painful? Isn't it simply lack of imagination, or at least our ability to suppress painful memories, that prevents us from being overcome by 'the horror' of the past? The overman accepts the idea of recurrence without the blinkers and filters that protect us from the pain of remembering. That is why Nietzsche believed the overman was so rare, and why the rest of us would react like Kurtz to the thought of history repeating itself again, and again, and again.

See also

20. Condemned to life
34. Don't blame me
65. Soul power
88. Total lack of recall

70. An inspector calls

When the health inspector visited Emilio's pizzeria and immediately closed it down, none of his friends could believe he had let it happen. After all, they said, he knew that an inspection was imminent, so why didn't he clean things up?

Emilio's answer was simple. He had been told that an inspector would be making a surprise call sometime before the end of the month. Emilio had sat down and wondered what day the inspection could be. It couldn't be on the 31st: if the inspector hadn't come before then, the inspection could only be on that day, and so it wouldn't be a surprise. If the 31st was ruled out, then so was the 30th, for the same reason. The inspection couldn't be on the 31st, so if it hadn't taken place by the 29th, that would only leave the 30th, and so it again would not be a surprise. But then if the inspection couldn't be on the 30th or 31st then it couldn't be on the 29th either, for the same reasons. Working backwards, Emilio eventually concluded that there was no day the inspection could take place.

Ironically, having concluded no surprise inspection was possible, Emilio was very unpleasantly surprised when the inspector walked through his door one day. What was wrong with his reasoning?

Source: The widely discussed 'surprise examination paradox' has its origins in a wartime Swedish radio broadcast

The short answer to this puzzle is that people in everyday life are not as particular in their choice of words as logicians. By 'surprise' the inspectors simply meant that they would not tell Emilio in advance which day the visit would be. If by the 31st only one possible day remained and the inspection would not be a complete surprise, so be it.

Many philosophers would say that this is an uninteresting answer, since it doesn't solve the problem but merely dissolves it in the vague soup of ordinary speech. But I think this response is ungenerous. It is always worth reminding ourselves that the ambiguities and grey areas of language are sometimes needed for us to make sense of the world, even though these same imprecisions can on other occasions get in the way of understanding.

Nevertheless, it is true that this answer leaves the hard problem unsolved. What if the promise of a surprise visit was meant quite literally, so that any resulting visit which was not a surprise, such as one that occurred on the 31st, would contradict the promise of a surprise visit?

Perhaps the idea of a surprise inspection is just incoherent. On this view, Emilio's reasoning was perfect, and what he concluded was true: there can be no surprise inspection. Therefore the announcement in advance of surprise inspection cannot be made without it implying some kind of contradiction.

The solution looks neat, but it is undermined by the fact that there obviously can be a surprise inspection, as Emilio found out, to his great cost. If the promise was made and was fulfilled, it seems hard to argue that it was incoherent.

There is also the intriguing possibility that the person who reasons there can be no surprise merely shifts the source of the surprise. On the 29th, for example, Emilio would have concluded that no surprise inspection could be made on the 30th or the 31st. But that still means an inspection, albeit not a surprise one, could be made on either of the two days remaining. And since he does not know which day of the two it will be, it would still be a surprise if it happened on the 30th.

Even an inspection on the 31st might still be a surprise since, having concluded no surprise inspection is possible on that day, if an inspection were nonetheless made, that would be a surprise.

What is perhaps most surprising of all, however, is that a puzzle that looks like a little linguistic trick proves to be much more logically complex than it at first appears.

See also

16. Racing tortoises
25. Buridan's an ass
42. Take the money and run
94. The Sorites tax

71. Life support

Dr Grey was depressed. One of his terminally ill patients was being kept on a life-support machine. Before she lost consciousness for the last time, she had repeatedly asked that the machine be switched off. But the hospital ethics committee had ruled that it would be wrong to take any action intended to shorten the life of a patient.

Grey disagreed with the committee and was disturbed that the wishes of the patient had been ignored. He also thought that holding off death with the machine was merely prolonging the agony of her friends and relations.

Grey stood looking mournfully at his patient. But then something odd happened. A hospital cleaner caught the power cable that led to the life-support machine and pulled it out from the socket. The machine emitted some warning bleeps. The cleaner, disturbed by the sound, looked at the nearby doctor for guidance.

'Don't worry,' said Grey, without hesitation. 'Just carry on. It's all right.'

And indeed for Grey it was now all right. For no one had taken any deliberate action to shorten the life of the patient. All he was doing by leaving the accidentally unplugged machine turned off was not taking any action to prolong it. He now had the result he desired without breaking the instructions of the ethics committee.

Source: *Causing Death and Saving Lives* by Jonathan Glover (Penguin, 1977)

There is clearly a difference between killing and letting die, but is this difference always morally significant? If in both cases the death was intended and the result of a deliberate decision, aren't the people who made the decision equally culpable?

In the case of Dr Grey, it does seem odd to make a sharp distinction between killing and letting die. He had wanted to flip the switch on the life support machine and let the patient die. In fact, he merely failed to plug the machine back in, with the same intention and the same result. If it would have been wrong to act to make the patient die, then surely it is equally wrong to fail to do something easy to stop the patient dying? Or to put it the other way round, if it is morally justifiable to let the patient die, surely it would have been equally justifiable to have turned off the machine.

Yet the laws on euthanasia do distinguish sharply between killing and letting die. This has the bizarre consequence that doctors can stop feeding a patient in a permanent vegetative state, effectively starving them to death, but they can't administer a lethal injection and kill them quickly. In either case, the patient has no awareness and would not suffer. Nevertheless, it is hard to see how starving could be seen as ethically superior to a swift and painless death.

It could be argued that, although there is not always a morally significant difference between killing and letting die, it is important for legal and social reasons not to sanction any deliberate killing. There are some ethical grey areas, such as this life-support machine case, but society needs rules and the best and clearest place to draw the line is on the boundary between killing and letting die. In a few hard cases this may mean we have unsatisfactory results, such as with the patient of Dr Grey. However, this is better than opening the door to deliberate killing by doctors.

Nevertheless, since it assumes the difference between killing and letting die is the best way to distinguish between ethical and unethical treatment of patients, this argument begs the question: why not make the basic principles those of minimizing suffering and respecting the wishes of patients?

Whatever we conclude, the case of Dr Grey shows that, from an ethical perspective, the distinction between killing and letting die is far from unproblematic.

See also

15. Ordinary heroism
29. Life dependency
53. Double trouble
89. Kill and let die

72. Free Percy

'Today, I have initiated proceedings against my so-called owner, Mr Polly, under article 4(1) of the European Convention on Human Rights, which declares that "No one shall be held in slavery or servitude."'

'Since Mr Polly captured me in Venezuela, I have been held against my will, with no money or possessions to call my own. How can this be right? I am a person just like you. I feel pain. I have plans. I have dreams. I can talk, reason and feel. You would not treat your own in this way. So why do you allow me to be abused so blatantly?

'The answer I hear is, "Because you're a parrot, Percy." Yes, I am indeed a parrot. But although your convention is on *human* rights, throughout it talks of "everyone" and by everyone it means "all people". What is a person? It used to be thought that only white people were truly persons. That prejudice at least has been defeated. Surely a person is any thinking intelligent being that has reason and reflection and can consider itself as itself. I am such a being. I am a person. To deny me my freedom purely on the grounds of my species is a prejudice no more justifiable than racism.'

Source: Book two, chapter XXVII of *An Essay Concerning Human Understanding* by John Locke (5th edn, 1706)

Listen too much to the optimists or pessimists about biological science and you may well come to believe that Percy is not such a distant possibility. Who knows when genetic engineering will make it possible to breed a species of super-intelligent parrots or, more likely, chimpanzees?

If and when we do, will we be producing people? 'Person' is not the same kind of category as 'human being'. The latter picks out a biological species, the former apparently something less physiologically specific. Consider how we react to intelligent aliens in science fiction, such as the Klingons in *Star Trek*. 'They are people too' seems to be not just a reasonable response, but the right one, whereas it would just be false to say 'They are humans too.'

From a moral point of view, which category is more important? Consider the morality of torturing a Klingon. 'That's OK, he's not human,' certainly seems to me morally outrageous, whereas 'Don't do that, he's a person' seems morally just.

If this line of reasoning is right, then not only should Percy fly free, but we should think again about how we conceive of ourselves and other animals. First, the idea that our moral significance lies in our nature as persons rather than as human beings fits well with the idea that our identity is determined not by our physical bodies but by those features of the self that are essential to being a person: thought, feeling and awareness. They are what we require to continue to exist as persons, not our bodies.

Secondly, Percy's point about racism suggests that 'speciesism' is a real possibility. Speciesism would occur whenever we use the fact that a creature is of a different biological genus to justify treating it differently, when that biological difference is morally irrelevant.

As a matter of fact, no other animal has enough of the characteristics of a person to qualify for protection under the European Convention of Human Rights. However, there are many animals that not only feel pain, but can to some extent remember and anticipate it. Could it not be argued that this in itself means we are morally obliged to take this pain into account and not cause it unnecessarily? And if we fail to do so, purely because the animals in question are not human, are we not guilty of speciesism? The charge needs to be answered, even though there is not much prospect of it making it to a court of law.

See also

5. The pig that wants to be eaten
32. Free Simone
54. The elusive I
65. Soul power

73. Being a bat

What is it like to be bat? Try imagining it. Perhaps you see yourself being very small, bat-shaped and hanging upside down inside a cave with hundreds of your friends. But that isn't even coming close. What you really seem to be imagining is you inhabiting the body of a bat, not *being* a bat. Try again.

If you're finding it hard, one reason is that, as a bat, you have no language, or if we are a little more generous, only a primitive language of squeaks and cries. It is not just that you have no public language to articulate your thoughts, you have no inner thoughts – at least not any that employ any linguistic concepts.

Another reason, perhaps the hardest part of all, is that bats find their way around by echolocation. The squeaks they emit work a little like radar, letting them know what objects are in the world by how the sounds rebound off objects and back to them. What is it like to experience the world in this way? It could conceivably be that the perceptions the bat has are just like our visual ones, but that would be very unlikely. A third reason, even more outlandish, is that the bat sees a kind of radar screen, like that in an aeroplane cockpit.

No, the most likely explanation is that to perceive the world through echolocation is to have a kind of sense experience totally different from that of a human being. Can you even begin to imagine that?

Source: 'What is it like to be a bat?' by Thomas Nagel, republished in *Mortal Questions* (Cambridge University Press, 1979)

The invitation to imagine the perceptual world of the bat was first made in a famous paper by the American philosopher Thomas Nagel called 'What is it like to be a bat?'. The difficulty – if not impossibility – of giving an answer is supposed to reflect an intractable problem in the philosophy of the mind.

The scientific study of the mind is really still, if not in its infancy, then certainly pre-pubescent. In many ways we now understand a great deal. In particular, there is no doubt that the mind depends upon a functioning brain and we have come a long way in 'mapping' the brain: identifying which regions are responsible for which functions of the mind.

But despite this, something called the mind–body problem still remains. That is to say, we know there is some kind of very intimate relation between the mind and the brain, but it still seems mysterious how something physical such as the brain can give rise to the subjective experiences of minds.

Nagel's bat helps to crystallize the problem. We could come to understand completely how the bat's brain works and how it perceives through echolocation, but this complete physical and neural explanation would still leave us with no idea of what it feels like to be a bat. Thus in an important sense we would be unable to enter the mind of the bat, even though we understood everything about how its brain worked. But how can this be, if minds depend on nothing more for their existence than functioning brains?

To put it in another way, minds are distinguished by the first-person perspective they have on the world. Every conscious creature perceives the world from the point of view of some 'I', whether it has the concept of self or not. But the physical world is characterised in purely third-person terms – everything in it is a 'he', 'she' or 'it'. That is why a description of a brain and how it works can be complete – because it includes everything that can be captured by a third-person point of view – yet leave out what seems to be most crucial to experience – the first-person point of view.

What does all this show? Is it that the mind will always elude a scientific explanation, because the points of view of consciousness and science are totally different? Or is it that we just haven't yet devised a framework for understanding the world scientifically that captures both first- and third-person points of view? Or is it that the mind simply isn't part of the physical world at all? The first possibility seems prematurely pessimistic; the second leaves us hoping for a way forward we cannot even being to comprehend; and the third seems to fly in the face of all we know about the close connection of mind and brain. Finding a way forward seems to be as difficult as thinking your way into the mind of a bat.

See also

13. Black, white and red all over
21. Land of the Epiphens
59. The eyes have it
68. Mad pain

74. Water, water, everywhere

NASA had dubbed it 'Twin Earth'. The newly discovered planet was not just roughly the same size as ours, it had a similar climate and life had evolved there almost identically. In fact, there were even countries where people spoke dialects of English.

Twin Earth contained cats, frying pans, burritos, televisions, baseball, beer and – at least it had seemed – water. It certainly had a clear liquid which fell from the sky, filled rivers and oceans, and quenched the thirsts of the indigenous humanoids and the astronauts from Earth.

When this liquid was analysed, though, it turned out not to be H_2O, but a very complex substance, dubbed H_2No. NASA therefore announced that its previous claim that water had been found on Twin Earth was wrong. Some people say that if it looks like a duck, walks like a duck and quacks like a duck, then it is a duck. In this case, the billed bird waddled and quacked, but it wasn't a duck after all.

The tabloid newspaper headlines, however, offered a different interpretation: 'It's water, Jim, but not as we know it.'

Source: 'The meaning of "meaning" by Hilary Putnam, republished in *Philosophical Papers, Vol. 2: Mind, Language and Reality* (Cambridge University Press, 1975)

Is H_2No water or not? More to the point, why should we care? Problems like these strike many as examples of philosophers' unhealthy preoccupation with matters of mere semantics. What does it matter whether we call H_2No water or not? We know what it is and what it is not.

It matters if you are interested in where meaning comes from. Most of us do not have an explicit theory of meaning, but we nonetheless do assume a rough-and-ready one. This is that the meanings of words are like definitions which we carry around in our heads. For instance, let's say I mistakenly believe that a migraine is just a bad headache. I might then say, 'I've got a terrible migraine.' If it is pointed out to me that I do not in fact have a migraine at all, I can admit my mistake, but I would still have a sense that I knew what *I meant* when I said I did. The mistake is a mismatch between the correct definition and the one I had internalised. What fixes the meaning of a word, on this account, is its definition, and definitions are the kinds of things that can be stored in minds as well as dictionaries.

The H_2No story, however, challenges this account. It should be clear that when earthlings and twin earthlings think 'This is water' they are having thoughts about two different substances. Earth water and Twin Earth water are not the same thing – they just happen to share the same name. Now, imagine Earth and Twin Earth 1,000 years ago. No one then knew what the chemical composition of water was. Thus, if you consider what would have gone on in the mind of someone thinking 'that is a glass of water', it would have been the same in the case of both the earthling and the twin earthling. But now imagine a person from each planet thinking this about the same glass of 'water'. If it is H_2No, the twin earthling would be having a true thought, but the earthling would be having a false one, since it isn't what we call water at all. But that means they can't be having the same thought, since the same thought cannot be both true and false.

If this line of reasoning is correct – and it does seem compelling – we are left with a surprising upshot. Since what is going on in the head of the earthling and twin earthling is exactly the same, but their thoughts are different, that means thoughts are not entirely in the head! At least part of a thought – that which supplies the meaning of the words – is actually out there in the world.

So the question of whether H_2No is water is not simply one of mere semantics. How you answer it determines whether meanings and thoughts are, as we usually assume, carried around in our heads, or outside of our heads, in the world. It can literally drive your thinking out of your mind.

See also

11. The ship *Theseus*
23. The beetle in the box
63. No know
68. Mad pain

75. The ring of Gyges

Herbert slipped the ring of Gyges on to his finger and was immediately startled by what he saw: nothing. He had become invisible.

For the first few hours, he wandered around testing his new invisibility. Once, he accidentally coughed and found that in the ears of the world, he was silent too. But he had physical bulk, and would leave an impression on a soft cushion or create an unexplained obstacle for those seeking to walk through him.

Once he became used to what it was like to live invisibly, Herbert started to think about what he could do next. To his shame, the ideas that popped into his head first were not entirely savoury. He could, for instance, loiter in the women's showers or changing rooms. He could quite easily steal. He could also trip up the obnoxious suits who shouted into their mobile phones.

But he wanted to resist such base temptations and so tried to think of what good deeds he could do. The opportunities here, however, were less obvious. And for how long could he resist the temptation to take advantage of his invisibility in less edifying ways? All it would take would be one moment of weakness and there he'd be: peeking at naked women or stealing money. Did he have the strength to resist?

Source: Book two of *The Republic* by Plato (360 BCE)

It is tempting to see the ring of Gyges as a test of moral fibre: how you would act under the cloak of invisibility reveals your true moral nature. But how fair is it to judge someone by how they would act when confronted by more temptation than most people could resist? If we are honest, imagining ourselves with the ring may reveal that we are disappointingly corruptible, but that is not the same as saying we are actually corrupt.

Perhaps what the mythical ring enables us to do is have sympathy with the devil, or at least some of his minor cohorts. Celebrities behaving badly, for example, attract our disapproval. But how can we imagine what it is like to have enormous wealth, endless opportunities for indulgence and sycophantic hangers-on ready to pander to our every whim? Can we be so sure that we too wouldn't end up disgracing ourselves?

Some insight into our current moral condition may be provided by considering how we would act with the ring at our disposal for a limited period. It is one thing to confess that, given time, we might give in to the allure of clandestine voyeurism; it is quite another to think that the first thing we'd do is head off down to the nearest gym's changing rooms. Someone who would follow that path is separated from actual peeping Toms only by fear or lack of opportunity.

The ring thus helps us to distinguish the difference between things we genuinely believe are wrong and those that only convention, reputation or timidity stop us from doing. It strips down our personal morality to its essence, removing the veneer of values we only pretend to hold. What we are left with might be distressingly thin. We probably wouldn't engage in random murder, but one or two loathed enemies might not be safe. Many feminists would argue that far too many men would use the opportunity to rape. We may not turn into career thieves, but property rights might suddenly look less inviolable.

Is that too pessimistic? If you ask people how they think others would behave with the ring and how they themselves would, you will often find a stark contrast. Others would turn into amoralists; we would retain our integrity. When we respond in this way, are we underestimating our fellow human beings, or are we overestimating ourselves?

See also

34. Don't blame me
54. The elusive I
66. The forger
85. The nowhere man

76. Net head

No more would Usha feel ill at ease in the company of her name-dropping, bookish colleagues. Confidently, she sidled up to the ostentatiously learned Timothy to test out her new powers.

'Usha, daaarling,' he said. 'How like *la belle dame* you look tonight!'

'"Full beautiful, a faery's child"?' replied Usha. 'I'm flattered. But, "Her hair was long, her foot was light, And her eyes were wild." I can't speak for my eyes, but my shoes are size eights and my hair is most definitely short.'

Timothy was clearly taken aback. 'I didn't know you were such a fan of Keats,' he said.

'To paraphrase Kant,' replied Usha, 'perhaps you have no knowledge of myself as I am, but merely as I appear.' And with that, she left him standing, aghast.

Her new implant was working a treat: a high-speed wireless chip that was connected to the world-wide web and a built-in encyclopaedia. It responded to the effort to remember by delving into these information sources and picking out what was being looked for. Usha could not even tell what she was actually remembering and what the chip had retrieved. Nor did she care, for now she was the most erudite person in the room, and that was what counted.

Usha is a cheat. There's no doubt about that. She is pretending that she has read and remembered things that in fact her amazing implant is bringing to her mind for the first time.

But does that mean she doesn't know what Keats and Kant wrote? The fact that she has an unorthodox way of accessing the information does not in itself show she doesn't have knowledge. What, after all, is the difference between accessing information stored in your brain and accessing information stored elsewhere, but directly connected to it?

The case is even more compelling if you accept, along with many philosophers, that knowledge is some kind of justified true belief. Usha's beliefs about Keats and Kant are true and she is as, if not more, justified in believing them to be true on account of the efficiency of her chip as we are to take what we remember to be true on account of the dubious efficiency of our brains.

Perhaps what is most interesting about this case is not the question of what Usha knows but what role remembered facts play in intelligence and wisdom. Usha's dazzling display did not just depend on her being able to access quotes: she had to use them with wit and understanding. It is this which marks her out as intelligent, not the ability to regurgitate classic poems and prose.

Yet the background to the story suggests we are sometimes fooled into thinking otherwise. Usha used to be intellectually intimidated because she was surrounded by people who were able to cite, quote and reference great works with ease. Do such people really display any great intelligence or merely an ability to recall? Note that Timothy may have started the conversation by evoking a Keats poem, but its eponymous heroine didn't actually look like Usha at all.

We may have other good reasons for thinking Usha's implant is no substitute for actually reading great books. It is only by spending time with a valuable work that you really understand it and think through what it means. Usha's plucked quotes lack any understanding of background and context. So while she may use them wittily to embarrass her colleague, were the conversation to turn to the nuances of Keats or Kant, she would probably be found wanting.

But, crucially, so might Timothy. The point is that knowledge alone of the contents of great works of philosophy and literature is not an indicator of wisdom or intelligence. A computer chip could be just as effective at storing such knowledge as a human brain. It's what we do with that knowledge that counts.

See also

3. The Indian and the ice
30. Memories are made of this
40. The rocking-horse winner
63. No know

77. The scapegoat

Why had Marsha joined the police force? In her own mind the answer was clear: to protect the public and to make sure justice was done. Those considerations were more important than following the rules.

She kept telling herself that, because she feared she lacked the resolve to break the rules in order to stay true to her ideals. A good man had made a terrible mistake, and an innocent woman was dead as a result. But by a sequence of accidents and coincidences, Marsha had enough circumstantial and forensic evidence to convict a different man of the crime. Not only that, but the man she could frame was a nasty piece of work who was certainly responsible for a number of murders. She had merely never been able to gather enough evidence to make the charges stick in court.

She knew that the due process of the law left no room for framing, but surely it would be better to get a repeat murderer behind bars than a man who posed no threat to anyone? The justice in that was greater than the injustice of denying a killer the benefits of a fair trial.

Source: *Insomnia*, directed by Christopher Nolan (2002)

'If anyone harmed my kids, I'd kill them.' That's not an unusual thing to hear otherwise law-abiding citizens say. But what are the people who say it thinking?

Some might explain that, although they know it would be wrong to take justice into their own hands, they are simply and honestly admitting how they would feel. Others might be less defensive. The person who harmed their children would deserve all they got. The law might come down against them, but natural justice would not.

It should be uncontroversial that the law and morality are not the same thing. That is why unjust laws are possible and civil disobedience is sometimes laudable. Nevertheless, the principle of the rule of law is an important one. Only in exceptional circumstances should we bend or break the rules. It is in the best interests of all of us that we forbid people from taking the law into their own hands, even if they do so for good motives.

These general considerations, however, are not much use to Marsha. She might entirely agree with this analysis, but her problem is whether or not these are the kinds of exceptional circumstances which warrant rule-breaking. How could she decide that?

Several different ways of determining this could vindicate her deceit. For instance, we might think that rule-breaking is permitted if three conditions are met. First, it must result in a significantly better outcome than rule-following. This would seem to be the case in Marsha's situation. Second, the action should not undermine rule-following in general. This condition would also be met, as long as Marsha's deceit remained secret. Third, the rule-breaking must be the only means of achieving the better outcome. It seems there is no other way in which Marsha could ensure the real menace ends up in prison.

There does then appear to be a plausible moral justification for Marsha's proposed deception. And yet the idea of a cop and not a court deciding who should be punished is a repugnant one.

There are good reasons for this: we need safeguards to prevent police officers abusing their powers, even if this sometimes means the guilty go free.

Can we have it both ways? Perhaps it is not contradictory to say that society must demand that the police always follow the rules, but that it is nevertheless sometimes good if they secretly break them. Our collective job may be to uphold the rule of law, but our individual duty may be to ensure we do what is best, inside or outside the law.

See also

7. When no one wins
17. The torture option
36. Pre-emptive justice
50. The good bribe

78. Gambling on God

And the Lord spake unto the philosopher, 'I am the Lord thy God, and though you have no proof I am who I say I am, let me give you a reason to believe that will appeal to your fallen state: a gamble based on self-interest.

'There are two possibilities: I exist or I don't exist. If you believe in me and follow my commands and I exist, you get eternal life. If I don't exist, however, you get a mortal life, with some of the comforts of belief. Sure, you've wasted some time at church and missed out on some pleasures, but that doesn't matter when you're dead. But if I do exist, eternal bliss is yours.

'If you don't believe in me and I don't exist, you have a free and easy life, but you will still end up dead and you won't live with the reassurance of belief in the divine. If I do exist, however, it's an eternity of hot pokers and torment.

'So, gamble that I don't exist and the best is a short life, while the worst is eternal damnation. But bet that I do exist, however unlikely that is, and the worst is a short life, but the best is eternal life. You'd be mad not to.'

Source: *Pensées* by Blaise Pascal (1660)

All around the world there are people who don't regularly worship, study religious texts or even follow their religion's teachings. Nonetheless, they don't give up belief in their God or gods altogether. For example, they still get their children baptised, arrange bar mitzvahs, or have a religious funeral. They may also pray in times of need.

Such people may not have reasoned as precisely as our gambling God, but the same basic principles underlie their behaviour: it's best to maintain at least minimal commitment to God, just in case. It is as much the reasoning of the insurance salesman as the gambler: it doesn't cost much in time and effort but it might just save your soul.

The wager makes sense only if there really are two possibilities, but, of course, there aren't. There are many gods to believe in and many ways of following them. Evangelical Christians, for example, believe that you will go to hell if you do not accept Jesus Christ as your saviour. So if you place your divine bet on Islam, Hinduism, Sikhism, Jainism, Buddhism, Judaism, Confucianism or any other religion, you still lose if Christ turns out to be king of heaven.

The stakes still remain the same, of course: eternal damnation is one possible outcome of making the wrong choice. But the problem now is that you can't insure against this highly improbable eventuality, because if you pick the wrong religion, you're damned anyway.

Perhaps you might think that the all-loving God wouldn't condemn people to hell for believing in the wrong religion, so any will do. But a God this kind and accepting of error would surely not damn atheists to the eternal flames either. The only God it is worth taking out insurance against is a fundamentalist one, and those policies are valid for one very specific deity only.

What is more, it is odd that a God who can see into the furthest reaches of our souls would accept a belief based on such shallow and calculating self-interest. Over time, perhaps you would come to genuinely believe and not just go through the motions. In religious devotion, practice makes perfect. But God would still recognise the insincerity that motivated your belief and judge you accordingly.

So the bet really needs to be stated more carefully. Your choice is between believing in one particular vengeful and punishing God, who commands belief in only one of the fundamentalist religions as opposed to the many more competing ones; or believing either that there is no God or that he is not so egotistical to demand that you believe in him before he'll offer you the opportunity to redeem yourself. And even if you bet on a nasty God, there are many to choose from, each of which will be most displeased that you chose someone else.

Betting turns out to be a mug's game after all.

See also

24. Squaring the circle
45. The invisible gardener
58. Divine command
95. The problem of evil

79. A Clockwork Orange

The Home Secretary had been told in no uncertain terms that his plan was 'politically unacceptable'. But just because it was similar to something a well-known novelist had described in a work of dystopic fiction, that was no reason to dismiss it out of hand.

Like the Ludivico process in Anthony Burgess's *A Clockwork Orange*, the new Crime Aversion Therapy programme took repeat offenders through an unpleasant, though not lengthy, treatment that left them repulsed by the very thought of the types of crime they had committed.

To the Home Secretary it seemed not so much a win–win situation, as a win–win–win one: the taxpayer won, as treatment was cheaper than prolonged and repeated imprisonment; the criminal won, as life was better outside than inside prison; and society won, because previously troublesome blights on the community were turned into law-abiding citizens.

And yet the civil liberties brigade bleated on about 'brainwashing' and denying the essential liberty and dignity of the individual – even though the programme was entirely voluntary. What, thought the Home Secretary, was there to object to?

Source: *A Clockwork Orange* by Anthony Burgess (Heinemann, 1962)

When people talk about dignity and liberty they can either be describing two of the most important landmarks on the ethical landscape or just uttering weasel words. When people complain that a new technology is an affront to the dignity of humanity, for example, they are as often as not simply expressing their own reflexive disgust at something unfamiliar and unusual. *In vitro* fertilisation, for example, was rejected by many when it was new, on the grounds that it reduced humanity to the level of a laboratory specimen. Now most people accept it as a welcome and effective treatment for fertility problems.

So we should be suspicious when people claim that something like Crime Aversion Therapy is an attack on human liberty and dignity. Perhaps they are simply expressing a prejudice against an innovation that shows that humans are not as mysterious as we would like to think, and that they too can be manipulated scientifically.

It could be argued that the therapy is only doing in a systematic way what usually happens haphazardly. Through a combination of socialisation and instinct, we learn to become repulsed by certain forms of behaviour. We shrink from hurting other people, not because we reason that it is wrong to do so, but because we come to feel that their pain is to be avoided. Sometimes, however, people fail to learn this lesson. Perhaps they lack the innate empathy that allows most of us to identify with the pain of others. Or maybe they have been desensitised to violence and have come to see it as good. In those cases, what is wrong with artificially instilling the instincts that nature or nurture failed to develop?

Talk of brainwashing is very powerful, but it seems that much of our behaviour is a kind of habit fostered by a combination of ongoing negative and positive reinforcement by parents and society at large. In effect, we are all slowly brainwashed from birth. It is only when brainwashing is done quickly, or with a result that we don't like, that it suddenly becomes ethically objectionable. Isn't Crime Aversion Therapy simply an accelerated and remedial version of the kind of unobjectionable brainwashing we usually call socialisation?

For similar reasons, we should be careful about overstating our claims to freedom. We do not think that a person freely refrains from violence only when they are as inclined to inflict it as not, but still choose not to do so. An ordinary, decent person *feels* rather than *chooses* some kind of aversion to inflicting unnecessary pain on others; it is not simply a matter of coolly exercising 'free will'. So if a therapeutic process merely instils what is for most people an ordinary level of aversion to criminal behaviour, how can that result in a person less free than you or I?

If there are good arguments against Crime Aversion Therapy, we need to go beyond a vague appeal to freedom and dignity.

See also

17. The torture option
35. Last resort
50. The good bribe
97. Moral luck

80. Hearts and heads

Schuyler and Tryne both sheltered Jews from the Nazis during the occupation of the Netherlands. They did so, however, for quite different reasons.

Tryne was a woman whose acts of kindness were purely spontaneous. Suffering and need spoke to her heart and she responded without thinking. Friends admired her generosity of spirit, but sometimes reminded her that the road to hell was paved with good intentions. 'You may feel moved to give money to a beggar,' they would say, 'but what if he then spends it all on drugs?' Tryne was unmoved by such worries. In the face of human need, all you can do is offer a hand, surely?

Schuyler, in contrast, was known as a cold woman. The truth was that she didn't really like many people, even though she didn't hate them either. When she helped others, she did so because she had thought about their plight and her duties, and concluded that helping was the right thing to do. She felt no warm glow from her good deeds, only a sense that she had chosen correctly.

Who of Schuyler and Tryne lived the more moral life?

People like Tryne are described as 'good', 'kind' or 'generous' more often than people like Schuyler. We sense that their kindness is deeply rooted in their personalities and flows naturally from them. The instinctiveness of their generosity suggests that the very essence of their being is good. In contrast, much as we can admire people like Schuyler, we do not *sense* their goodness in the same way. At best, we may learn to admire their willingness to submit to what they see as their duties.

It is interesting that we should respond in that way. For if morality is about *doing* the right thing, it is far from obvious that we should think Tryne is more morally praiseworthy than Schuyler. Indeed, as has been suggested, in her guileless way Tryne is perhaps more likely to do the wrong thing than Schuyler. For example, when travelling in Africa, you will frequently be asked by children for pencils, or sometimes money. Tryne would surely give. But Schuyler would probably think a little more, and conclude, along with most development agencies, that this kind of giving encourages dependence as well as feelings of inferiority and helplessness. It is far better to give directly to a school, and preserve the dignity of those you want to help.

There is a second reason to temper one's praise of Tryne. Since her actions are unthinking, isn't it just a matter of luck that she tends to act well? Why should we praise someone for just happening to have a generally good set of dispositions? What is worse, unless we reflect on our feelings, might not our instincts lead us astray? Think, for instance, about the many people in history who have shared Tryne's basic personality, but who have been brought up in racist cultures. Such people were often as unthinking in their racism as they were in their kindness.

Maybe we could go further. Schuyler deserves *more* moral credit precisely because she acts well *in spite of* her lack of instinctive empathy and compassion. Whereas Tryne's kindness requires no particular effort, Schuyler's is a triumph of human will over natural inclination.

However, reversing our instinctive judgement and seeing Schuyler as the more morally praiseworthy creates different problems. After all, doesn't it seem odd to say that the person whose goodness is more intimately enmeshed in their personality is less virtuous than the one who does good only because they reason that they should?

The trite solution to the dilemma is simply to say that goodness requires a marriage of head and heart, and that, while both Tryne and Schuyler manifest some facets of virtue, neither provides the model of the well-rounded, ethical individual. This is almost certainly true, but it avoids the real dilemma: is it how we feel or how we think that is more important in determining whether we are morally good human beings?

See also

17. The torture option
18. Rationality demands
50. The good bribe
83. The golden rule

81. Sense and sensibility

The humanoids of Galafray are in many ways just like us. Their sense perception, however, is very different.

For example, light reflected in the frequency range of the spectrum visible to humans is smelled by the Galafrains. What we see as blue, they sniff as citrus. Also, what we hear, they see. Beethoven's Ninth Symphony is for them a silent psychedelic light show of breathtaking beauty. The only things they hear are thoughts: their own and those of others. Taste is the preserve of the eyes. Their best art galleries are praised for their deliciousness.

They do not have the sense of touch, but they do have another sense we lack, called mulst. It detects movement and is perceived through the joints. It is as impossible for us to imagine mulst as it is for Galafrains to imagine touch.

When humans first heard about this strange race, it did not take long for someone to ask: when a tree falls in a forest on Galafray, does it make a noise? At the same time, on Galafray they were asking: when a film is shown on Earth, does it make a smell?

Source: *A Treatise Concerning the Principles of Human Knowledge* by George Berkeley (1710)

The conundrum 'If a tree falls in a deserted forest, does it make a sound?' is one of the oldest in philosophy. Because it has become so hackneyed, it is useful to be able to reconsider the problem from a new angle. Hence the curious question, 'When a film is shown on Earth, does it make a smell?' For, bizarre though it may sound, this question is just as pertinent as the classic one about the forest.

The puzzles arise from the realisation that how we perceive the world depends as much, if not more, on our constitutions as the world itself. It just so happens that airwaves of a certain frequency are translated by our brains into sounds. Dogs hear things that we do not, and there is no logical reason why other creatures couldn't translate these same waves into smells, tactility or colours. Indeed, synesthesia – sensory crossover, in which colours are heard or sounds seen – occurs in humans either permanently as a rare condition or temporarily, induced by hallucinogenic drugs such as LSD.

Given these plain facts, the question arises as to whether such things as sounds exist in the absence of creatures who hear. It is certainly the case that the air vibrates when a tree falls in an empty forest. But if sounds are in the ears of the hearers, isn't it the case that with no ears there are no sounds?

If you want to resist this conclusion and say that when a tree falls on Galafray it does make a sound, surely you also have to say that, by the same logic, when a film is shown on Earth, it does make a smell. For to say the tree makes a sound does not mean that anyone hears anything. It can only mean that events occur such that, if a person were present, they would hear a sound. And that is enough to justify the claim that there is therefore a sound made. But if this is true, why isn't it also the case that films smell? This is not the claim that when the film is shown anyone smells anything. All it means is that, if a person who smelled what we saw were present, they would smell the film. That seems to be as true as the claim that, if a human were in the Galafrayan forest when the tree fell, they would hear something.

This line of reasoning would seem to lead to the absurd conclusion that the world is filled with noises no one hears, colours no one sees, flavours no one tastes, textures no one feels, as well as a host of other sense experiences we cannot even imagine. For there is no end to the ways in which creatures might possibly perceive the world.

See also

21. Land of the Epiphens
28. Nightmare scenario
59. The eyes have it
73. Being a bat

82. The freeloader

Eleanor was delighted with her new broadband connection. Having been used only to dial-up, she loved the fact that now her internet connection was always on, and also that surfing and downloading was so much quicker. And it was a bonus that it happened to be completely free.

Well, to say it was free was perhaps a little misleading. Eleanor paid nothing for the service because she was using her neighbour's WiFi connection, otherwise known as a wireless Local Area Network. This enabled any computer within a limited range, as long as it had the right software and hardware, to connect without cables to a broadband internet connection. It so happened that Eleanor's apartment was close enough to her neighbour's for her to use his connection.

Eleanor didn't see this as theft. The neighbour had the connection anyway. And she was using only his excess bandwidth. In fact, a neat piece of software called Good Magpie made sure that her use of the connection never slowed her neighbour down by more than a negligible amount. So she got the benefits of his connection, but he didn't suffer as a result. What could be wrong with that?

Lots of people with WiFi capabilities on their laptops or handheld devices 'borrow' bandwidth on an occasional, *ad hoc* basis. Needing a connection on the go, they walk the streets looking for a wireless LAN signal, and then stop and collect their email. The companies or individuals whose connections they use never know, nor suffer any drop in performance as a result.

Eleanor is engaged in something much more systematic. She is using her neighbour's connection as her everyday means of accessing the internet. He pays while she plays. That seems extremely unfair. But Eleanor's actions do not have any bad effect on her neighbour. He has to pay for his connection anyway, and her usage doesn't interfere with his. Looked at in that light, Eleanor is no more a thief than someone who uses the shade cast by a tree in a neighbour's garden.

This is a particular example of the freeloader problem. Freeloaders take the benefits of the actions of others without contributing to them. Sometimes, freeloading diminishes the total sum of the benefits available, and in these cases it is not hard to see why freeloading is wrong. But on other occasions, the freeloader is, in effect, enjoying a surplus benefit and not taking anything away from anyone.

There are countless examples of such freeloading. A community organises a free concert in the park, which someone comes across by chance and enjoys at the very edge of the crowd, depriving nobody of their pleasure. But she makes no donation to the costs when the bucket comes round. Someone else illegally downloads from the internet a song which they would never buy. The artist is not deprived of any income since, had she been forced to pay, the downloader wouldn't have bothered. But she nevertheless enjoys the song.

If freeloading is a crime, it seems to be a genuinely victimless one. What then is wrong with it? Perhaps the key is not to focus on individual instances of freeloading, but patterns of behaviour. For example, we may not care that someone uses our WiFi connection, if it is understood that we might use other people's in the same circumstances. Similarly, it might be fine to pay nothing for a free concert you stumble across, if you make voluntary contributions to others you set out to visit. As long as there is as much give as take in the long run, freeloading itself is unobjectionable.

In Eleanor's case, however, it is all take and no give. She is not offering to host the connection herself some time in the future. She is therefore not freeloading in the spirit of mutual co-operation which would make her usage acceptable. Her actions manifest a lack of thought for others. Still, even if we think this is a little selfish, isn't it still true to say that her wrongdoing is very minor? In fact, wouldn't any condemnation stronger than saying that she's been a bit cheeky indicate that we had allowed ourselves to get too uptight about a completely harmless theft?

See also

14. Bank error in your favour
34. Don't blame me
44. Till death us do part
60. Do as I say, not as I do

83. The golden rule

Constance had always tried to observe the golden rule of morality: do as you would be done by, or, as Kant rather inelegantly put it, 'Act only on that maxim through which you can at the same time will that it should become a universal law.'

Now, however, she is sorely tempted by something that would seem to go against that principle. She has the chance to run off with the husband of her best friend, taking their entire family fortune with them. On the face of it, that would not be doing as she would be done by.

But, she reasoned, things are more complex than that. When we lock up a criminal, we are not saying we should also be locked up. We are saying that we should be locked up *if we were in the same circumstances as the criminal.* That proviso is crucial: context is all.

So, the question she should be asking herself is this: can she 'will that it should become a universal law' that people in her circumstances should run off with their best friend's husband and fortune? Put like that, the answer seems to be yes. She's not saying adultery and asset-stripping are usually good, only that in her specific circumstances they are. So that's settled then: she can run away with a clear conscience.

Sources: *The Analects of Confucius* (5th century BCE); *Groundwork for the Metaphysics of Morals* by Immanuel Kant (1785)

The golden rule of Confucius has emerged in various forms in virtually all the major ethical systems humankind has devised. In its simplicity it seems to offer a moral rule of thumb that we can all follow.

The problem Constance's situation highlights is not just a sophistical joke at the rule's expense. It goes to the heart of what the principle actually means. For either one of two extreme interpretations, the principle is either ridiculous or empty.

If it means that we should never do to anyone else what we would not have done to ourselves, no matter what the circumstance, then we would never do anything unpleasant, such as punish or restrain. Since we would object to being locked up ourselves, we would not lock up serial murderers. That is a nonsense.

That is why Constance is right to see that circumstances have to come into it. But because every circumstance is slightly different, every case is in some sense unique. So anything we did could be justified on the grounds that we would agree to be treated in the same way in *exactly* the same circumstance. But then the universal aspect of the golden rule vanishes and the rule becomes empty.

So, should we look for the middle path? This would have to involve some idea of *relevant similarity*. We should do as we would be done by in any situation which, though not exactly the same, is similar in the morally relevant ways. So, for example, although all unlawful killings are different, they are all relevantly similar in respect to the key moral issues.

Something like this approach has to be taken for the golden rule to work, but what we now have is far from a simple, transparent rule at all. For identifying relevant similarities is not an easy task, and it is not just those looking for excuses for wrongdoing who might claim a crucial relevant difference. Human affairs are extremely complex and if we fail to attend to the particularities of each case, we risk failing to do justice to them.

And so we come back to Constance. Her justification looks self-serving. But what if Constance's best friend actually turned out to be a lying cheat who had already siphoned off thousands of pounds from her family's bank account? What if she were making her husband's life hell? Under those circumstances, Constance's decision looks more like an act of heroism than selfishness.

Constance's dilemma reflects a challenge for anyone trying to observe moral principles: how to balance the need to follow general principles with the equally important need to be sensitive to the particularities of each situation.

See also

18. Rationality demand
44. Till death us do part
80. Heads and hearts
91. No one gets hurt

84. The pleasure principle

It's just typical – you wait years for a career breakthrough then two opportunities turn up at once. Penny had finally been offered two ambassadorial positions, both at small South Sea Island states of similar size, geology and climate. Raritaria had strict laws which prohibited extra-marital sex, drink, drugs, popular entertainments and even fine food. The country permitted only the 'higher pleasures' of art and music. Indeed, it actually promoted them, which meant it had world-class orchestras, opera, art galleries and 'legitimate' theatre.

Rawitaria, by contrast, was an intellectual and cultural desert. It was nonetheless known as a hedonists' paradise. It had excellent restaurants, a thriving comedy and cabaret circuit, and liberal attitudes to sex and drugs.

Penny did not appreciate having to choose between the higher pleasures of Raritaria and the lower ones of Rawitaria, for she enjoyed both. Indeed, a perfect day for her would combine good food, good drink, high culture and low fun. Choose she must, though. So, forced to decide, which would it be? Beethoven or Beef Wellington? Rossini or Martini? Shakespeare or Britney Spears?

Source: *Utilitarianism* by John Stuart Mill (1863)

In which of these odd little countries is it easier to live a good life? You might think that it is merely a question of preference. Let the art lovers go to Raritaria and the party animals to Rawitaria.

Those who like a bit of both – which is most of us – have to decide what they prize the most, or at least what they would find it easier to live without.

If it is simply a matter of taste and disposition, however, then why do the higher pleasures attract government subsidies when the lower ones are more often than not heavily taxed? If the pleasure we gain from listening to a Verdi opera is worth no more than the pleasure of listening to Motörhead, then why aren't seats at rock gigs subsidised as much as those at the Royal Opera House?

Thoughts such as these have led many to conclude that there is something superior about the 'higher' pleasures of the intellect and refined aesthetic appreciation. However, if this view is challenged, it is hard to come up with a justification for the higher/lower distinction. The suspicion is that this is just preference, snobbery or elitism dressed up as an objective judgement.

The problem exercised John Stuart Mill, the utilitarian philosopher, who thought that the goal of morality was to increase the greatest happiness of the greatest number. The problem he faced was that his philosophy seemed to value a life full of shallow and sensual pleasures above that of a life with fewer, but more intellectual ones. The contented cat would have a better life than a troubled artist.

The solution was to distinguish between the quality as well as the quantity of pleasure. A life full only of lower pleasures was worse than one with even just a few higher ones. This still leaves the problem of justification: why is it better?

Mill proposed a test. We should ask what competent judges would decide. Those who had tasted both higher and lower pleasures were the best placed to determine which were superior. And as the labels 'higher' and 'lower' suggest, he knew how he thought they would choose.

If Mill is right, Penny, as a competent judge, would choose Raritaria. She might regret the loss of lower pleasures, but the inability to experience the higher ones would bother her more. And her opinion carries more weight than that of those who have never appreciated high art, or those who have never indulged in baser pleasures. Would Penny actually decide this way, though? And would her judgement really tell us something about the general superiority of higher over lower pleasures?

See also

7. When no one wins
20. Condemned to life
26. Pain's remains
52. More or less

85. The nowhere man

'Your honour, my client's defence is very simple. He accepts that he did indeed write in his newspaper column that "the current manager of the England football team is a liar, an idiot and a national disgrace". He also accepts going on to say that he "should be shot". But by doing so, he in no way libelled the plaintiff, Mr Glenn Robson-Keganson.

'The reason for this is easy to see. At the time the article was written and published, there was no such person as the England football team manager. Mr Robson-Keganson had tendered his resignation two days earlier, and his offer had been accepted. This news became public knowledge on the day the defendant's article was published.

'The plaintiff claims that the accusations my client made were false. But they were neither true nor false, since they were not about anyone. Indeed, it would be more accurate to say they were meaningless. "Flar-Flar is a racehorse" is true if Flar-Flar is a racehorse, false if she is not, and meaningless if there is no such beast.

'The jury should therefore dismiss the case. It is just nonsense to suggest one can libel someone who does not exist. I rest my case.'

Source: 'On Denoting' by Bertrand Russell, in *Mind* 14 (1905), widely anthologised and republished on the internet

Logicians are not like ordinary people. When most people speak they are content that they can make themselves understood and that others will generally know what they mean, even if they put things a bit awkwardly or imprecisely at times. Logicians, on the other hand, are frustrated by the vagaries and ambiguities of everyday language. The point is, they will insist, that their apparently trivial quibbles have implications.

Consider the defence for the case brought by Glenn Robson-Keganson. The jury would probably dismiss it on the grounds that we know who he meant by 'the current manager of the England football team'. But let us take his words literally and accept that there was no such person at the time. Wouldn't they still insist that the allegations were false? For if there was no such person, to claim he was 'a liar, an idiot and a national disgrace' is surely untrue?

If we hold this, however, there are indeed implications, ones that greatly troubled Bertrand Russell when he pondered the truth of the statement 'the present king of France is bald' if Gaul is a republic. The problem is that, in logic, the negation of a false statement is true. So, for example, if 'the sun orbits the Earth' is false, then clearly 'the sun does not orbit the Earth' is true. That means, however, that if 'the King of France is bald' is false, then 'the King of France is not bald' must be true. But it can't be true that the King of France is not bald, because there is no such monarch. And so it seems that such statements as 'the King of France is bald' when there is no king and 'the current manager of the England football team is a liar' when there is no such manager are neither true nor false.

If a statement is neither true nor false, doesn't that make it meaningless? You might think so, but surely the meaning of the statement 'the current manager of the England football team is a liar' is perfectly clear. And a meaningless statement, the meaning of which is clear, would seem to be a contradiction in terms.

And so the implications of the apparently innocuous puzzle of how and whether such statements can be true or false spin out and multiply. We haven't even touched on the link with the idea that words correspond to objects in the world, and that the truth or falsity of statements depends on whether the correspondence holds.

The puzzle cannot, of course, be resolved here. One thing is clear, however. If you find these problems trivial rather than engrossing, don't study logic or the philosophy of language.

See also

23. The beetle in the box
45. The invisible gardener
47. Rabbit!
74. Water, water, everywhere

86. Art for art's sake

Marion was used to the inconvenience of discovering archaeological remains during construction projects. But nothing had prepared her for this.

The day they found the shaft, a message was delivered to her explaining what it contained. At the bottom of the shaft was a sealed box, containing a Michelangelo statue. The box was booby-trapped in several ways: opening it would set off a bomb; it contained a gas, which if exposed to oxygen, would explode; and other ingenious traps were built in. The upshot was that the artwork could never be revealed, as any attempt to do so or to move the box would destroy it.

But such a dangerous time-bomb could not be left underneath what was to become a hospital. So there seemed to be only two solutions: abandon the hospital and leave the work of art secure but unseen, or destroy it safely.

In the circumstances, there appeared to be little choice for Marion but to order the bomb squad in to conduct a controlled explosion. But she couldn't help thinking that it would be better for the statue to remain intact, even if no one could ever see it.

Most of us think that works of art have value, and not just in the monetary sense. Great works of art are worth preserving, and individuals and governments pay huge sums of money to acquire, restore or preserve them.

Are they valuable in themselves though, or does their value lie in what they do for those who observe them? It is tempting to think that they are valuable in themselves: Michelangelo's *David* would be no less of an artistic achievement if no one had ever seen it. Even if a never-seen or never-to-be-seen *David* would be a great work of art, what would be the point of its existence? It may have benefited its creator in some way, but after he died, for whom or what is the point of a work no one can admire?

Making the distinction between the quality of the work and the point of its existence is crucial to seeing Marion's dilemma, for there is little doubt that the statue in the box is an artwork of some quality. What is at issue is whether there is any point in such an artwork existing if no one can see it.

The preservers will say that the world is a better place by virtue simply of the statue existing. Those calling for demolition will counter that this is absurd: the world is improved because of the effects artworks have on those who view them. If people cannot feed on art, it serves no purpose. You may as well close our national galleries for ever and say that it is good enough that the paintings and sculptures within them exist. Nor would it matter that paintings are kept out of sight in private collections or museum safe rooms. To which the preservers will reply, the fact that it is better that people get to see art than not does not mean that unseen art has no value at all. An open gallery is better than a shut one, but a shut one is better than no gallery at all.

The nagging doubt remains: don't we need appreciators of art for art to have any value? Imagine another scenario: a deadly virus wipes out life on Earth, and there is no more life in the universe. The world is left full of art, but with no one to see it. If *David* were to fall off his plinth and shatter into a million pieces, would this desolate world really be any worse than it was when his marble gaze looked out on to it? If we tend to think it would, is that only because we imagine ourselves there and so insert into the thought experiment a consciousness which is supposed to be absent from it? Are we not making the mistake of those who look upon a corpse and imagine it still to be the person who has already ceased to exist?

See also

12. Picasso on the beach
37. Nature the artist
48. Evil genius
66. The forger

87. Fair inequality

John and Margaret went shopping to buy Christmas presents for their three sons: Matthew, aged fourteen, Mark, who is twelve, and Luke, ten. The loving parents always tried to treat their children equally. This year, they had budgeted to spend £100 on each of them.

For once it looked as if their shopping would be trouble free, for they soon found what they were looking for: hand-held PlayBoy games consuls at £100 each. Just as they were about to take three to the checkout, John noticed a special offer. If you bought two of the new, top of the range PlayBoyPlusMax consuls at £150 each, you would get an original PlayBoy free. They could spend the same amount of money and get superior goods.

'We can't do that,' said Margaret. 'That would be unfair, since one of the boys would be getting less than the others.'

'But Margaret,' said John, excited at the thought of borrowing his sons' new toys, 'how can it be unfair? This way none of them gets a worse gift than he would have done, and two of them do better. But if we don't take the offer, two of the kids are worse off than they would otherwise be.'

'I want them all to be equal,' replied Margaret.

'Even if it means making them worse off?'

Source: *A Theory of Justice* by John Rawls (Harvard University Press, 1971)

Many hold equality to be desirable, but few now accept that equality is to be pursued at all cost. This is because there seems to be something wilfully perverse about achieving equality by levelling down. We could easily make everyone equal simply by making everyone as poor as the poorest person in society. But that seems obviously to be a foolish thing to do because it doesn't help anyone. The poorest remain just as poor as they were and everyone else is harmed.

However, just because we accept that it may not always be worthwhile to impose equality, that doesn't mean we should simply accept all inequality without question. What we need to ask is when inequality is acceptable. John's explanation to Margaret about why they should treat their sons differently provides one answer. Inequality is permitted when no one is worse off as a result, but some people are better off.

This is very similar to what the political philosopher John Rawls called the 'difference principle'. In essence, this says that inequalities are permitted only if they are to the benefit of the least well off. However, it is not clear whether this applies to Matthew, Mark and Luke. Under the original gift plan, they form a classless micro-society in which each is the best and worst off. The plan to get the PlayBoyPlusMax deal does indeed make two of the least well off better off, but it is no help at all to the other one. So is it true to say that the plan is to the benefit of the least well off as a whole?

Of course, there are important differences when the principle is applied in the political and familial arenas. In society at large, John's argument seems intuitively persuasive. Within families, however, there may be reasons to place a higher priority on equality, since in very small groups, inequalities are felt more keenly and can lead to tensions.

This same consideration, however, does extend to the political domain. For one reason to be against inequality is precisely the effect it has on social cohesion and the self-esteem of the poor. As social psychologists have pointed out, even though materially people are no worse off if their neighbours get rich at no financial cost to themselves, psychologically they can be harmed by their increased awareness of the wealth gap between them. Seeing equality and inequality solely in material terms could thus be a terrible mistake, both in politics and in families.

See also

7. When no one wins
10. The veil of ignorance
22. The lifeboat
55. Sustainable development

88. Total lack of recall

Arnold Conan had just made an unpleasant discovery: he wasn't Arnold Conan at all. Or rather, he used not to be. It was all rather confusing.

This is the best sense he could make of his unusual autobiography. He was born Alan E. Wood. Wood was, by all accounts, a deeply unpleasant man: egotistical, selfish, cruel and ruthless. Two years ago, Wood had got into deep trouble with the State Bureau of Investigation. He was given a choice: spend the rest of his life in maximum security prison, where they would make sure he was victimised by the other inmates; or have his memory erased and replaced with that of an entirely fictitious creation of the spooks at the SBI. He chose the latter. And so it was that Alan E. Wood was put under a general anaesthetic, and when he woke up, he had forgotten all about his life to date. Instead, he remembered an entirely fictitious past, that of Arnold Conan, the man he now believed he was.

Conan had established that these were the facts. But he still did not know who he was: Wood or Conan?

Sources: *Total Recall*, directed by Paul Verhoeven (1990); 'We Can Remember It For You Wholesale' by Philip K. Dick, in *The Collected Short Stories of Philip K. Dick*, Vol. 2 (Carol Publishing Corporation, 1990)

As identity crises go, Conan/Wood's is about as bad as it gets. It seems he is either someone deeply unpleasant he knows nothing about or the fictitious creation of the security agencies. He is unlikely to want either possibility to be the truth.

Many people's initial intuition is that Conan is *really* Alan E. Wood. This is understandable. Our identity usually follows that of our brains and bodies. Since the life of the organism named Alan E. Wood at birth has continued uninterrupted, and there is no other person with a claim to his name walking the Earth, it would seem that Conan is Wood. After all, if he isn't Wood, where is Wood? Show us the corpse: no one has been killed.

The case may also be strengthened by the knowledge that Arnold Conan is a creation of agents and neurologists. Whatever he remembers of his childhood, for example, never really happened. Conan seems as unreal as Wood does real. So can there be any doubt that Conan is Wood, albeit mentally altered beyond all recognition?

In Conan/Wood's mind, certainly. For whatever the logic of our reasoning dictates, he feels like Conan, not Wood. He would not, for example, experience any desire to have his old self restored. Indeed, he might be horrified by the idea that he would once again become the amoral man he once was.

Before we say that he is simply in denial about the truth, consider that he has lived as Conan for two years; not all his past is fictitious. Consider also how people can suffer widespread amnesia. If you received a bump on the head and lost all memories of your past up until two years ago, you would certainly be changed by the experience, but you would not be transformed into someone else entirely.

So it is not hard to see how Conan/Wood could be seen as being Wood. It is just that Conan has existed only for a few years, and all his memories of before that time are false. The fact that he started out as an artificial creation does not negate the fact that he has lived for two years as a real human being.

If the case can be made both ways, how are we to decide which is most persuasive? If we ask different questions, we will get different answers. Do Wood's friends recognise him as the man they knew? Who does Conan's new wife think she has married? What would Wood's debtors claim? Who does Conan/Wood think he is? Rather than asking what the facts are, perhaps we should ask which of these questions matters the most, and so which answer is the one we should accept.

See also

2. Beam me up . . .
30. Memories are made of this
54. The elusive I
65. Soul power

89. Kill and let die

Greg has just one minute to make an agonising choice. A runaway train is hurtling down the track towards the junction where he is standing. Further down the line, too far away for him to reach, forty men are working in a tunnel. If the train reaches them, it is certain to kill many of them.

Greg can't stop the train. But he can pull the lever that will divert it down another track. Further down this line, in another tunnel, only five men are working. The death toll is bound to be smaller.

But if Greg pulls the lever, he is deliberately choosing to bring death to this gang of five. If he leaves it alone, it will not be him who causes deaths among the forty. He must bring about the deaths of a few people, or allow even more to die. But isn't it worse to kill people than it is simply to let them die?

The rails are humming, the engine noises getting louder. Greg has only seconds to make his choice. To kill or let die?

Source: 'The Problem of Abortion and the Doctrine of Double Effect' by Philippa Foot, republished in *Virtues and Vices* (Oxford University Press, 2002)

Greg's dilemma sometimes elicits strong intuitions either way. For some, it seems obvious that he must pull the lever. By doing so he will almost certainly reduce the death toll, and that is surely what any reasonable, moral person must do.

For others, if Greg pulls the lever he is placing himself in the position of God, deciding who is to live and who is to die. Certainly, we should try to save lives, but not if we can do so only by killing others. If we justify killing by the other lives it saves, we are on a slippery slope.

The problem with this second line of reasoning is that it seems Greg is choosing who will die whether he pulls the lever or not. He is not electing to take on God's role, he has had it thrust upon him. The important point is not whether he acts or does not act, but that it is within his power to act or not act and that either way he must take responsibility for his choice.

Isn't it true that we are just as responsible for what we could easily have done but chose not to do, as we are for what we do? If I know a glass of water is poisoned and I see you going to drink it, am I not as responsible for your death if I let you go ahead as I would be if I encouraged you to drink up? If I see a child wandering on to a busy road and I walk on by, when I could easily pull her back on to the pavement, am I not at least partially responsible for her death? And isn't it misguided to say that Greg would be responsible for the deaths of the workers on the line if he pulled the lever but without any responsibility at all if he doesn't?

And yet if we don't make some moral distinction between killing and letting die, aren't there more uncomfortable repercussions? Most obviously, if we think it is all right for doctors to allow people who are terminally ill to die rather than prolong their lives against their wishes, why isn't it also all right to assist them to an easy and painless death, should they request it? Less obvious, but even more striking, is the claim that we are responsible for the deaths of people in the developing world, whom we allow to die for lack of water, food and medicines we could quite easily give them without great cost to ourselves.

If claiming that there is a world of difference between killing and letting die seems unreasonable, to counter that there is no difference at all creates a whole new set of moral dilemmas.

See also

15. Ordinary heroism
29. Life dependency
53. Double trouble
71. Life support

90. Something we know not what

George Bishop stared intently at the bowl of oranges before him and then thought it into thin air.

He started by making an obvious distinction between the features of the oranges that are mere appearances and those properties that they really have. The colour, for example, is a mere appearance: we know that the colourblind, or animals with different physiologies, see something very different from the normal human experience of 'orange'. The tastes and smell are also mere appearances, as these too vary according to who or what is perceiving the fruit, while the fruit itself remains the same.

But as he started stripping away the 'mere appearances' from the fruits, he found himself left with vanishingly little. Could he even talk about the actual size and shape of the fruits, when these features seem to depend on how his senses of sight and touch perceive them? To truly imagine the fruit in itself, independent of the mere appearances of sense perception, he was left with the vague idea of something, he knew not what. So what is the real fruit: this gossamer 'something' or the collection of mere appearances after all?

Source: *The Principles of Human Knowledge* by George Berkeley (1710)

It doesn't take much reflection to open up the distinction between appearances and reality. As infants, we are 'naive realists', assuming the world is just as it appears. As we grow up we learn to distinguish between the way things appear to our senses and the way they really are. Some of these – such as the difference between things which are genuinely small and those which are merely far away – are so obvious that they are scarcely remarked upon. Others, such as the way in which the taste or colour of a thing varies according to the perceiver, we know, even though in everyday life we ignore or forget it.

As we develop a basic scientific understanding of the world, we probably come to see this difference in terms of the underlying atomic structure of objects and the way in which they appear to us. We may be dimly aware that this atomic structure itself is explained in terms of sub-atomic structure, but we need not bother ourselves with the details of our current best science. All we need to know is that the way things appear is a function of the interplay between our senses and the way they really are.

All this is little more than mature common sense, but it is a common sense that glosses over some important details. Reality has been distinguished from appearances, yet we don't have a clear idea what this reality is. No problem, you may think. The intellectual division of labour means that we leave this job to the scientists.

Is it not the case, though, that scientists are as much in the world of appearances as we are? They too study what is presented to our five senses. The fact that they have instruments that allow them to examine what is not visible to the naked eye is a red herring. When I look through a telescope or microscope I am as stuck in the world of appearances as I am when I see with unaided vision. Scientists are not looking beyond the world of appearances; they are merely looking at that world more closely than we ordinarily do.

This is a philosophical, not a scientific problem. We seem to understand the difference between the world of appearances and the world as it is, but it seems impossible to get behind appearances and see this 'real' world. When we understand that the moon is far away, not tiny, or that the stick in water is not bent, we are not getting beyond appearances, we are merely learning how some appearances are more deceptive than others.

This leaves us with a dilemma. Do we remain committed to the idea of a world beyond appearances, and accept that we have no idea what this world is, and can't even imagine how we might come to know it? Or do we give up on the idea and accept that the only world we can live in and know is the world of appearances after all?

See also

28. Nightmare scenario
51. Living in a vat
81. Sense and sensibility
98. The experience machine

91. No one gets hurt

Scarlett could not believe her luck. For as long as she could remember, Brad Depp had been her heart-throb. Now, amazingly, she had stumbled across his secluded holiday home in the Bahamas, which not even the paparazzi knew about.

What is more, when Brad saw the solitary walker on the beach, he had offered her a drink, and as they talked he turned out to be as charming as she had imagined. And then he admitted that he had got a bit lonely these last few weeks, and although, because of his lifestyle, it would have to remain a secret, he would very much like it if she were to spend the night with him.

There was just one problem: Scarlett was married to a man she very much loved. But what you don't know can't hurt you, and he would never know. She would get a night of fantasy and Brad would get a little comfort. Everyone would be either as they were or richer for the experience. No one would suffer. With so much to gain and nothing to lose, what earthly reason could there be for Scarlett to resist Brad's fabulous come-to-bed eyes?

If someone trusts you, what is lost if you betray that trust? As Scarlett is tempted to see it, sometimes nothing at all. If her husband remains ignorant of her tryst, then his trust in her will remain intact. 'No one gets hurt' runs her reasoning, so why not go ahead?

It may sound cold, it may sound calculating, but such ways of thinking are common. Things that we would usually consider wrong can appear perfectly acceptable, just as long as we are sure that no one is harmed. So, for example, a person who would never rob a bank will happily accept a large pay-out from a malfunctioning ATM, reasoning that the bank won't miss the money and no individual will suffer as a consequence.

Is this really the best way to determine the morality of our actions: tot up the consequences in terms of happiness and misery and go with whatever course of action increases the former and minimises the latter? The system has the merit of simplicity, but it also seems to gloss over some of the subtler dimensions of our moral lives.

Consider the nature of trust. Many people would say that mutual trust is one of the most important things in their close personal relationships. Most of the time we would know straight away if this trust has been betrayed. If we trust someone to spend our money wisely, for example, we soon find out if they have blown it on something useless. This is trust, but it is not the deepest kind, because we do not just rely on trust to make sure our wishes are respected: we can see if they haven't been.

The deepest trust, in contrast, is precisely the willingness to place our faith in someone even when you could not tell whether they had kept their word or not. This is the kind of trust that dispenses with the safety net of openness or disclosure. Such trust is essential if we are to be secure in fidelity, for, as we all know, infidelities can often be kept secret, sometimes for ever.

So if Scarlett has her night of passion with Brad, she will have broken the deepest trust of all. The fact that her husband would never know is precisely what makes her betrayal a profound one, for to be trusted in such circumstances is to be trusted as deeply as is possible.

And yet, 'no one gets hurt'. Trust may have been broken, but trust is not flesh and bone. How can it be that Scarlett harms no one, yet shatters the most important part of her most treasured relationship?

See also

7. When no one wins
34. Don't blame me
44. Till death us do part
83. The golden rule

92. Autogovernment

It is crazy to think that in the bad old days, ministers who perhaps knew very little about economics were trusted to make important decisions about such matters as spending and taxation. It was some improvement when the power to set interest rates was transferred to central bankers. But the real breakthrough came when computers became good enough to manage the economy more efficiently than people. The supercomputer Greenspan Two, for example, ran the US economy for twenty years, during which time growth was constant and above the long-term average; there were no price bubbles or crashes; and unemployment stayed low.

Perhaps unsurprisingly, then, the leader in the race for the White House, according to all the (computer conducted and highly accurate) opinion polls is another computer – or at least someone promising to let the computer make all the decisions. Bentham, as it is known, will be able to determine the effects of all policies on the general happiness of the population. Its supporters claim it will effectively remove humans from politics altogether. And because computers have no character flaws or vested interests, Bentham will be a vast improvement on the politicians it would replace. So far, neither the Democrats nor the Republicans have come up with a persuasive counter-argument.

The idea of letting computers run our lives still strikes most of us as a little creepy. At the same time, in practice, we trust ourselves to computers all the time. Our finances are managed almost entirely by computers, and nowadays many people trust an ATM to log their transactions accurately more than a human banker. Computers also run light railways, and if you fly you may be unaware that for long periods the pilots are doing nothing at all. In fact, computers could easily handle landings and take-offs: it's just that passengers can't yet accept the idea of them doing so.

So the idea that computers might run the economy is not so fanciful. After all, most economists rely heavily on computer models and predictions already. It is a small step from acting on the information generated by machines to letting the machines do the acting for us.

Could a computer ever replace politicians altogether? This is the more radical proposal of Bentham's presidential campaign. If a computer could calculate the effects of policy on the happiness of the population, why couldn't it then simply do what would please us the most?

Dispensing with humans altogether is not so easy. The problem is that the goals need to be set for the computer. And the goal of politics is not simply to make as many people happy as possible. For example, we have to decide how much inequality we are prepared to tolerate. One policy might make more people happy overall, but at the cost of leaving 5 per cent of the population in wretched conditions. We might prefer a slightly less happy society where no one has to live a miserable life.

A computer cannot decide which of these outcomes is better; only we can do that. What is more, it is probable that the outcome we desire will change according to circumstances. For example, the richer a society becomes, the more intolerable it may be to allow anyone to go without the bare essentials. Also, the richer we become, the more we might think we are obliged to help other, less prosperous countries.

Even if the computer knew what we wished, that doesn't end the debate. For should a democratic society simply follow the will of the majority or should the opinions of the minority also be taken into account? If so, how so?

The day may well come, perhaps sooner than we think, when computers will be able to manage the economy and even public services better than people. But it is much harder to see how they could decide what is best for us and send all politicians packing for ever.

See also

9. Bigger Brother
10. The veil of ignorance
36. Pre-emptive justice
87. Fair inequality

93. Zombies

Lucia lived in a town where the lights were on, but nobody was ever home. She lived among zombies.

This was not as scary as it might sound. These zombies were not the flesh-eating ghouls of horror films. They looked and behaved just like you and I. They even had exactly the same physiology as you and I. But there was one key difference: they had no minds. If you pricked them they would say 'ouch' and wince, but they felt no pain. If you 'upset' them they would cry or get angry, but there would be no inner turmoil. If you played them soothing music they would appear to enjoy it, but in their minds they would hear nothing. On the outside, they were ordinary humans, but on the inside, nothing was going on.

This made them easy to get along with. It was easy to forget that they didn't have inner lives as she did, since they spoke and behaved just like ordinary people and that included references to how they felt or what they thought. Visitors to the town would also fail to notice anything strange. Even when Lucia let them in on the secret, they refused to believe her.

'How do you know that they have no minds?' they would ask. 'How do you know that other people do?' would be Lucia's reply. That usually shut them up.

'How do you know?' is often a very good question. It is also, alas, one it is very hard to answer conclusively. We rarely, perhaps never, know beyond any doubt whatsoever. The best we can hope for is to have good reasons for what we believe. Better reasons, at least, than those for believing the contrary. That is why we don't feel we need to worry about the possibility that we are living among zombies. Even if it is possible that we are, as long as we have more reasons to believe that we aren't, we can safely avoid fretting over improbable possibilities.

The reasons for thinking other people aren't zombies are principally ones of economy. If they walk like us, talk like us and have brains and bodies like us, then the chances are they are like us in all significant respects, including how things feel to them from the inside. It would be very odd if the nervous system which gives me consciousness didn't do the same for others.

This, however, is precisely the point at which the zombie possibility becomes interesting. For why should we think that physical similarities are indicative of mental ones? The problem of consciousness is precisely that it seems inexplicable that purely physical entities such as brains should give rise to subjective experiences. Why should a C-fibre firing in the brain feel like anything at all? What has that brain event got to do with the sensation of pain?

If these questions seem serious and without satisfactory answers, then it would follow from them that there is nothing logically contradictory in imagining brain events such as C-fibres firing without any concomitant sensation. In other words, the idea of zombies – people just like us in every physical respect, but who have no inner lives at all – is perfectly coherent. And so the possibility that other people are such zombies, however improbable, is a real one.

As in horror films, killing off the zombies is no easy task. In order to discount the possibility of their existence, you need to show why it is that a creature that has the same physiology as us must also have the same basic psychology. That means, for example, showing why C-fibre firing must feel like pain, rather than seeing the colour yellow, or nothing at all. It's a challenge that so far no one has been able to meet to the general satisfaction of philosophers. Until someone does, we cannot be sure that zombies do not walk the Earth.

See also

19. Bursting the soap bubble
32. Free Simone
39. The Chinese room
68. Mad pain

94. The Sorites tax

A Party Political Broadcast by the Chancellor of the Exchequer, Lord Sorites.

These are taxing times for our country. The last government left us with run-down public finances and the need to raise extra revenue. But you, the people, do not want to have to foot the bill. So how can we raise the money we need without making you feel the pain?

The answer is simple. Focus groups, opinion polls and economists have shown that charging an extra 0.01 per cent tax has a negligible effect on personal income. No one who is comfortably off is made to struggle, no one rich is made poor, no one already struggling is made to struggle more, by paying 0.01 per cent extra on their tax bill.

So today we are raising income tax by 0.01 per cent. And logically, since this small amount makes as little difference to the person who earns 0.01 per cent less than you as it does to you, we can repeat the step tomorrow, when you are in the position of that insignificantly poorer person. And so the next day, and the next, for the next 300 days.

Each time we raise taxes, we do so in a way that makes no difference to your quality of life. And so your quality of life will not be affected. Yet, miraculously, the net effect of these measures will be a large increase in government revenue, which we intend to use to cut the national debt and still have enough change left to buy everyone in the country a drink. We hope you will use it to toast our ingenuity.

Source: The ancient Sorites paradox, attributed to Eubulides of Miletus (4th century BCE)

A politician who made a speech like this should not expect to win any votes by so doing. Even if your maths isn't up to calculating that he is actually proposing a tax rise in excess of 3 per cent, no one would be fooled that 300 tiny tax rises don't add up to a major hike.

Yet the logic of the Chancellor is hard to fault. It follows that of the ancient Sorites paradox. In the original, we are asked if removing a grain of sand from a heap can ever transform the heap into a non-heap (a small pile, perhaps). The answer seems to be no. But that means you could keep removing a grain of sand, one by one, until you had only one left, and that would still be a heap.

One solution appears to be that somewhere along the line, removing a grain of sand does mean that we no longer have a heap. But that just seems absurd. Hence the paradox: if one grain makes a difference, that is absurd; if it doesn't, a single grain can be a heap, which is just as absurd.

Our tax example suggests a way out. Could we not argue that each small increment does make a difference, although it is just a small difference? Clearly, if you add up several small differences you can end up with a big one.

This does not, however, get to the heart of the problem. The paradox is that no tiny change in income can be enough to make the difference between someone being well-off or struggling. The paradox is precisely the contrast between what is obvious when we 'zoom out' and see the cumulative effect of small changes and when we 'zoom in' and see each one having no effect at all.

When confronted by this paradox, most people are convinced it's just a linguistic trick or there is some other sleight of hand at work. The puzzle should be taken more seriously, however. Many argue that the way out requires us to accept the vagueness of many concepts, such as rich and poor, tall or short, heap or pile. The problem with that solution is that, if we allow too much vagueness into language and logic, reason itself becomes vague. The alternative – that tiny changes really can make the difference between being rich and being poor – preserves the rigour of logic and language, but seemingly at the cost of realism.

See also

16. Racing tortoises
25. Buridan's an ass
42. Take the money and run
70. An inspector calls

95. The problem of evil

And the Lord spake unto the philosopher, 'I am the Lord thy God, all-loving, all-powerful and all-knowing.'

'Surely not,' replied the philosopher. 'I look at this world and I see horrible disease, hunger, starvation, mental illness. Yet you don't stop it. Is it that you can't? In which case, you are not all-powerful. Is it because you don't know about it? In which case you are not all-knowing. Or perhaps you don't want to? In which case you are not all-loving.'

'Such impudence!' replied the Lord. 'It is better for you if I don't stop all this evil. You need to grow morally and spiritually. For that you need the freedom to do evil as well as good, and to confront the chance occurrence of suffering. How could I possibly have made the world better without taking away your freedom to grow?'

'Easy,' replied the philosopher. 'First, you could have designed us so that we felt less pain. Second, you could have made sure we had more empathy, to prevent us doing evil to others. Third, you could have made us better learners, so we didn't have to suffer so much to grow. Fourth, you could have made nature less cruel. Do you want me to go on?'

Source: The problem of evil recurs in different forms throughout the history of theology

Could God have made a world in which there was less suffering but in which we had the same opportunities to exercise our free

will and, as the religious put it, grow spiritually? It is difficult to answer this question without simply pandering to our prior prejudices. For atheists, the answer is obviously yes. The philosopher in our story makes four suggestions straight away. None of these seems impossible. Consider that a certain amount of empathy comes naturally to us, and that makes most of us less willing to harm others. If that is compatible with us having free will, why would having more empathy threaten it?

Consider also that our ability to learn is also something we have no direct control over. Indeed, some of us are better at it than others. Why couldn't God have made us all better learners, so we could understand why things were right or wrong without the need to be exposed to terrible evil? Considerations such as these lead many to conclude that God could very easily have created a world in which there was less suffering. That he did not do so is proof that he either doesn't exist or is not worthy of our worship.

But if you do believe in God, these arguments can seem very weak. For who are we to say that God could have done a better job? If God exists he is infinitely more intelligent than us. So if he created a world full of suffering, he must have done so for good reasons, even if those reasons elude our pathetic minds.

As a response this can seem unsatisfactory. For what it adds up to is the claim that, if ever we are presented with rational reasons to doubt the existence of God, we simply have to accept that our intellects are finite and that what might seem irrational or contradictory does make sense from the divine point of view. But that just means dismissing the role of rationality in religious belief. And you can't have it both ways. It's no use defending your belief using reason on one occasion, if you don't accept that a reasoned argument against belief has any force.

This is where the problem of evil seems to leave the believer.

The best rational attempts to resolve the problem are all effectively versions of the argument that it must be all for the best in the long run. But to accept that requires a faith that defies reason, for our best reason tells us this is not the best that God could have done. If the atheists can be accused of claiming to know better than God, believers can be accused of knowing better than reason. Which is the more serious charge?

See also

8. Good God
17. The torture option
18. Rationality demands
58. Divine command

96. Family first

Sally's boat was one of only a few that regularly sailed these waters, which is why she always made a point of listening out for SOS calls. So when she heard that an explosion had left a dozen people in the ocean, without lifeboats, she immediately set a course for them.

But then she received a second message. Her own husband's fishing boat was sinking and he needed help too. The problem was that, to get to him, she would need to go even further from the drowning dozen. And with the weather turning bad, and no other vessels responding to the distress calls, it seemed clear to Sally whoever she went to second would probably be dead by the time she got there.

There was not much time to think. On the one hand, not to save her husband would seem to be a betrayal of their love and trust. On the other, he was a good man, so wouldn't he also see the sense in saving twelve people instead of just one? She knew where she wanted to head first, but not where she should.

It has been held by most ethicists that morality demands the equal respect of all persons. As Jeremy Bentham said, 'Each person is to count for one and no one for more than one.' That, however, seems to conflict with the strong intuition that we have a special responsibility towards family and close friends. Surely, for example, parents should put the welfare of their own children above that of others?

Not so fast. Parents do have a special responsibility to their own offspring. That means they are required to make sure they are well fed, for example, whereas they are under no obligation to monitor the nutritional intake of other children. Is that the same as saying that they should put their own children's welfare *above* that of others?

Consider, for example, when there is competition for places at a good school. If there is only one place available for two potential students, then each set of parents is responsible for making a good case that it should be for their own child. But for the process to be fair, each case should be considered on its merits and the welfare of both children taken equally into account. If any parent tried to interfere with these basic principles of fairness, they would be behaving wrongly. They would have crossed the line between acceptable and laudable parental concern for their offspring and a lack of respect for the welfare of others.

The basic principle at work here seems to be that we are right to focus our energies and attention on family and friends rather than strangers, just as long as by doing so we treat everyone fairly.

As principles go, however, it's not a very useful guide to practice. Is it fair to lavish expensive toys on your own children while others starve to death? Is it fair for articulate, knowledgeable parents to get the best out of public services while other, usually poorer, ones fail to take full advantage of what is on offer? Is it fair to help your children with their homework and so enable them to do better than kids whose parents are not willing or able to do the same?

Some of these questions are more difficult than others. But unless you believe that we need think only of ourselves and our families, such dilemmas will arise for everyone at some stage. Sally's dilemma is particularly acute, for lives are in immediate danger. But the same question she must ask presents itself to us all:

am I justified in putting the welfare of those close to me above that of others?

See also

27. Duties done
29. Life dependency
89. Kill and let die
97. Moral luck

97. Moral luck

Mette looked into the eyes of her estranged husband, but could find no flicker of remorse.

'You tell me you want us back,' she said to him. 'But how can we do that when you won't even admit that you did the wrong thing when you left me and the children?'

'Because in my heart I don't think I did wrong, and I don't want to lie to you,' explained Paul. 'I left because I needed to get away to follow my muse. I went in the name of art. Don't you remember when we used to talk about Gauguin and how he had to do the same? You always said he had done a hard thing, but not a wrong one.'

'But you are no Gauguin,' sighed Mette. 'That's why you're back. You admit you failed.'

'Did Gauguin know he would succeed when he left his wife? No one can know such a thing. If he was in the right, then so was I.'

'No,' said Mette. 'His gamble paid off, and so he turned out to be right. Yours didn't, and so you turned out to be wrong.'

'His *gamble*?' replied Paul. 'Are you saying luck can make the difference between right and wrong?'

Mette thought for a few moments. 'Yes. I suppose I am.'

Source: The eponymous essay from *Moral Luck* by Bernard Williams (Cambridge University Press, 1981)

Luck can mean the difference between success and failure, happiness and misery, riches and poverty, but surely it can't separate the virtuous from the bad? Whether we are good, decent human beings must depend on who we are and what we do, not what happens beyond our control.

That's what common sense would suggest. But even if luck isn't the main determinant of moral goodness, can we really be so sure that it has no role at all to play in ethics?

Most fundamentally, there is what is known as constitutive luck. We are born with certain traits and characteristics, and these are developed by the way we are brought up. However, we don't choose any of this. The result is that, by the time we become old enough to make our own choices, we may already be more or less predisposed towards good or evil than our average peers. A person who reaches this age who finds themselves liable to fly into violent rages is therefore more likely to do wrong, purely as a result of drawing an unlucky ticket in the lottery of genetics and upbringing.

Even if we set aside constitutive luck, we are still familiar with the sentiment, 'there but for the grace of God go I'. We are probably all capable of doing more wrong than we do, and it is partly a matter of luck if we manage to avoid finding ourselves in the circumstances where our darker sides come to the fore.

In the case of Paul and Mette, the role of luck is even more pronounced. Mette's argument is that two people can behave in exactly the same way, unsure of what the outcome will be, and that only when we know if that outcome is good or bad can we say if the person did right or wrong. So a Gauguin who leaves his family and becomes a great artist has made the morally right choice, whereas Paul, who made the same choice but without success, is to be condemned for doing wrong.

If that seems an outlandish example, just consider how we are all careless from time to time. If that carelessness results in a serious injury, for example, the person who made the slip is seen as morally culpable. If, by chance, our lack of attention has no bad consequences, few will think much worse of us. Does that suggest there is such a thing as moral luck? Or should we condemn more those whose poor judgements happily have no bad effects? Should we say that Gauguin was in the wrong, even though we think that, on balance, it is much better that he did what he did than stayed with his family?

See also

27. Duties done
34. Don't blame me
43. Future shock
96. Family first

98. The experience machine

Robert had been sitting in front of the consent form for two hours and still he did not know whether to sign it or shred it. His choice was between two futures.

In one, his prospects were bleak and the chances of realising his dreams slim. In the other, he would be a famous rock star guaranteed to be kept permanently happy. Not much of a choice, you might think. But whereas the first life would be in the real world, the second would be entirely within the experience machine.

This device enables you to live the whole of your life in a virtual-reality environment. All your experiences are designed to make you happier and more satisfied. But crucially, once in the machine you have no idea that you are not in the real world, nor that what is happening to you has been designed to meet your needs. It seems you are living an ordinary life in the ordinary world: it is just that in this life, you are one of the winners for whom everything seems to go right.

Robert knows that once he is in the machine, life will be great. But still, something about its phoniness makes him hesitate to sign the form that will take him to this paradise.

Source: Chapter 3 of *Anarchy, State, and Utopia* by Robert Nozick (Basic Books, 1974)

It's easy to see why Robert is holding back. Life in the machine would be bogus, inauthentic, unreal. But why should an authentic 'real' life, with its remorseless cycles of ups and downs, be preferable to a bogus happy one?

A sales agent for the happiness machine could offer some powerful arguments that it is not. First, consider what 'authenticity' and 'real' mean. An authentic person is who they really are, not what they pretend to be. But Robert will still be Robert in the machine. He can reveal his true personality there as easily as he can outside it.

Then you might say that in the real world, you become a rock star by merit, whereas in the machine it would not be his own efforts which were rewarded. To which it might be replied, have you heard most rock stars? Talent has little to do with it; luck and opportunity everything. Robert's fame in the machine will be no less deserved than the fame of the countless wannabes who make it up the slippery pole of pop. Indeed, that is the great recommendation of the experience machine. Success in life depends so much on luck: were you born in the right place, at the right time, to the right parents? Were you endowed with the abilities your society values and rewards? Did you have access to the people and places that could help you get ahead? To say it is better to leave yourself at the mercy of Lady Luck when you could choose to be happy is crazy.

As for the idea that you would be abandoning the real world, we might say: get real. The world you live in now is no more than the sum of your experiences: what you see, hear, feel, taste, touch, smell. If you think it is more real because it is caused by sub-atomic processes rather than silicon chips, perhaps you need to reconsider your notion of reality. After all, even our concept of the world of science *beyond* experiences is ultimately based on observations and experiments wholly *within* the world of experience. So in some sense, reality is just appearances.

And yet we still might not want to enter the machine, determined as we are that our futures should be as much a product of our own will and efforts as possible. If we persist with this refusal to enter the machine, then at least one thing must be true: when we consider what is in our own best interests, we care for more than just happiness. Otherwise, we would enter the machine like a shot.

See also

1. The evil demon
19. Bursting the soap bubble
28. Nightmare scenario
51. Living in a vat

99. Give peace a chance?

The emissary had been sent by Hitler under the utmost secrecy. If the British ever tried to reveal the nature of his mission publicly, Berlin would deny all knowledge of the trip and denounce him as a traitor. But that would surely not be necessary. No one could see how Churchill could refuse the deal he had to offer.

Hitler knew that Churchill wanted to avoid needless casualties. Both leaders realised that a conflict between the two nations would cost countless thousands of lives. But war could be averted. Hitler was offering guarantees that, once the Final Solution was completed, no further offensives would be launched and only insurgents within the lands he occupied would be killed. That would certainly mean there would be fewer lives lost than if Britain attempted to liberate France and overthrow the Nazi regime in Germany.

The Führer was sure this would appeal to the leader of the country that had invented utilitarianism. After all, who could prefer a course of action that would lead to more deaths over one that would lead to fewer?

Although no such mission was in fact undertaken during the Second World War, Hitler did believe at various points that Britain would accept a peace deal that would allow him to keep the territories he had conquered. Perhaps one reason for this was precisely the thought that, since war would cost more in human lives, peace would look like the best option, both pragmatically and morally.

There are many, especially those who lost relatives in the concentration camps, who would shudder at the mere thought of such a deal. The proposal seems to buy peace with the lives of the innocent victims of the Holocaust.

If you share this response, then think very carefully about how you judge the morality of other wars. A lot of the debate about the ethics of military intervention is conducted in terms of the human cost of action or inaction. For example, anti-war campaigners are quick to point out that it is estimated that in the first year after the invasion of Iraq in March 2003, around 10,000 civilians had been killed. However, Saddam Hussein is believed to have killed 600,000 civilians during his time in power. In response, there are those who argue that UN sanctions, not Saddam's regime, were responsible for the deaths of half a million Iraqi children. And many more numbers are traded in an attempt to justify or condemn going to war.

All this seems to assume that if a war costs more lives than it saves, then it is morally wrong. But on this logic, it is easy to imagine a scenario, such as the secret offer of a deal from Hitler, which would have made it better for the allies to have left Europe to fascism.

One reason why many think this is unacceptable is that the concentration camps are an evil that seems to demand a response. It may be that it would cost more lives to end the genocide than the action would save, but it is not tolerable to allow such wickedness to go unchecked. Our humanity is more precious than our individual human lives.

Even if we factor out the Holocaust, there are still reasons to prefer bloody liberation to bloodless toleration. People choose to risk their lives for their ideals because they think some values are more important than mere survival. Hence the saying that it is better to die a free man than live as a slave. That is why, during the first Gulf war at least, many Iraqis rejoiced even as bombs fell all around them. The morality of war is a thorny issue and one that cannot be resolved by a simplistic totting up of lives lost and lives saved.

See also

17. The torture option
18. Rationality demands
35. Last resort
79. A Clockwork Orange

100. The Nest café

Eric was a regular at the Nest café. The quality of the food and drink was unexceptional, but they were remarkably cheap.

One day he asked the manager how she did it. She leaned over and whispered, conspiratorially, 'Easy. You see, all my staff are from Africa. They need to survive but can't get regular jobs. So I let them sleep in the cellar, feed them just enough, and give them £5 cash a week. It's great – they work all day, six days a week. With my wage bill so low, I can offer low prices and make handsome profits.

'Don't look so shocked,' she continued, reading his reaction. 'This suits everyone. They choose to work here because it helps them, I make money, and you get a bargain. Top up?'

Eric accepted. But perhaps this would be his last coffee here. Despite the manager's justification, he felt, as a customer, he would be complicit in exploitation. As he sipped his americano, however, he wondered if the staff would appreciate his boycott. Weren't these jobs and the shelter of the cellar better than nothing?

You don't have to be a militant anti-capitalist to recognise that everyone who lives in a developed country is essentially in the same position as Eric. We import comparatively cheap goods because those producing them work for a pittance. And if we know this yet carry on buying, we are helping to maintain the situation.

Do not be fooled by the superficial differences. Eric is closer to the cheap labour than we are, but geographical proximity is not ethically significant in this case. You don't cease to exploit someone simply by putting miles between you. Nor is the illegality of the café staff the issue. Simply imagine a country where such employment practices are permitted.

You might say that what is a fair wage depends on what is normal locally. So 'slave wages' in a country like Britain could be very generous in Tanzania. That is true, but it doesn't end the debate. For the crucial point is that the Nest café takes advantage of the need of its workers to pay them as little as possible. The injustice isn't primarily about comparative pay, but the mercenary indifference towards the welfare of the workers. In the same way, people growing coffee in the developing world may be no worse off than many of their compatriots, but that doesn't mean their western paymasters need not care that they work so hard for so little, when we can well afford to pay them more.

Nor does the 'it's better than nothing' defence cut much ice. The alternative isn't nothing, it's more pay or better conditions. A boycott may put an exploited worker out of a job, but conversely competition from businesses such as the Nest café means properly paid workers elsewhere lose theirs.

So it seems that in all morally relevant respects, we are indeed in the same position as Eric. If he is wrong to help feather the Nest, we are wrong to buy from businesses that treat the people at the end of their supply chains in the same way.

This is a very troubling conclusion, for it makes almost every one of us complicit in exploitation. This may seem so outrageous that it might be considered evidence that the argument has gone awry. But that would be a complacent response. Historically, there have been many systemic injustices which whole sectors of society have implicitly supported. Consider the actions of most whites in South Africa during apartheid, the middle and upper classes during the time of slavery, men before women were given equal rights. It is possible for almost all of us to do the wrong thing all the time. If Eric should reconsider where he buys his coffee, so should we, and many other things besides.

See also

7. When no one wins
22. The lifeboat
34. Don't blame me
44. Till death us do part

Index

Index